"LIFE'S NOT FAIR, BUT GOD IS GOOD."

That simple statement has developed into a book—this book. "Life's not fair, but God is good!"

Yes He is. God is good. He doesn't create the problems—He redeems them. He doesn't make the mistakes—He fixes them. He doesn't cause cancer. He heals. He doesn't kill dreams or bodies. He gives life. He gives the big picture—the ability to see beyond this temporal set-back to a glorious comeback!

You can be a living, loving testimony that life's not fair—but God is good!

LIFE'S NOT FAIR, BUT GOD IS GOOD

ROBERT H. SCHULLER

BANTAM BOOKS
NEW YORK · TORONTO · LONDON · SYDNEY · AUCKLAND

*This edition contains the complete text
of the original hardcover edition.*
NOT ONE WORD HAS BEEN OMITTED.

LIFE'S NOT FAIR, BUT GOD IS GOOD

*A Bantam Book/published by arrangement
with Thomas Nelson Publishers*

PUBLISHING HISTORY
*Nelson edition published 1991
Bantam edition / June 1993*

ISBN 0-553-56167-7

Published simultaneously in the United States and Canada

Bantam Books are published by Bantam Books, a division of Bantam Doubleday
Dell Publishing Group, Inc. Its trademark, consisting of the words "Bantam Books"
and the portrayal of a rooster, is Registered in U.S. Patent and Trademark Office
and in other countries. Marca Registrada. Bantam Books, 1540 Broadway, New
York, New York 10036.

PRINTED IN THE UNITED STATES OF AMERICA

OPM 15 14 13 12 11 10 9 8

CONTENTS

*Life's
Not Fair,
but God
Is Good*

CHAPTER ONE

———— • ————————————————————— • ————

"Life's Not Fair!"
—YOU HEAR IT
EVERYWHERE.

Young and old, rich and poor, fast and slow, tall and short, men and women, boys and girls—all have seen and felt life's cruel injustices. Whoever you are, wherever you've come from, you have heard these words— "LIFE'S NOT FAIR!"

ON THE PLAYGROUND

The sting of cruelty starts early. Its roots can be found in early childhood experiences.

I speak from personal experience. Like every other boy, I have lived through the suffering of choosing teams for a baseball game. You know what I'm talking about. Two boys, usually the strongest and the most athletic, appoint themselves captains. Then those two captains take turns choosing who they want on their team. Of course, they choose the best players first. Like all sporting organization heads, they want to win, and their draft choices reflect their opinions of the various players.

I cannot tell you how painful it is to wait on the sidelines, waiting, waiting, waiting, hoping to be picked. The big captains pick one boy, then another, then another. Meanwhile, they pass over you. You are not as good. You arc less desirable. You are worth less. Life's not fair!

I know that pain, for I was always the last one to be picked. I can still hear the haunting words, "Oh, no! We got stuck with Schuller!"

I'm not the only one who has felt the pain of cruelty in my childhood. Every day, millions of children go through it. Stand a while on the sidelines of a playground. Watch the children as they play ball and chase each other. Listen to their squeals of laughter as they play. On the surface they seem to be having fun. However, if you listen and observe closely, you'll see that the play soon becomes competitive. Good-natured give-and-take evolves quickly into cut-throat competition. Before long the loser declares, *"That's not fair!"*

At the Stadium

We grow up. Or do we?

"Take me out to the ballgame!" How thrilling it is to go to the stadium—hot dogs, cold drinks, peanuts. The roar of the crowd. Boys in summer. Everybody loves that all-American sport—baseball. Fans are fiercely loyal. They are also very fickle. They pay a lot to see their favorite players play. And they expect a lot. Just watch a well-paid athlete drop an easy catch and listen to the derisive comments.

The fans are happy as long as their team is winning. The sports commentators and the national television cameras create a great deal of pressure for these professional athletes. This game, which was once upon a time played for fun, has now become a crucial contest. It is worth millions.

As the end of the season approaches, the pressure mounts more than ever. Wins and losses are carefully tabulated. The tension fills the air. The fall classic is approaching. Will our favorite team be in it? The pitcher throws out the first pitch. The crowd roars. The game proceeds. One up, one down, so it goes. No score. Suddenly the pitcher throws a bad pitch. "Ball!" Three balls later, he has walked his first batter.

A man on first. He tries to steal to second on the next pitch. "OUT!"

You've all seen these scenes many times at the stadium or on TV. The manager runs out to argue with the umpire, chest to chest. What's he saying? It's probably best not repeated, but you can be sure that in the midst of all the fury you will hear these three words, *"That's not fair!"*

IN THE OFFICE

Linger by the water cooler at any office building. Watch the men and women who visit briefly before they return to their desks. What are they feeling? What are they saying? Oh, sure they are friendly. They have to work together. There is a sense of *camaraderie*. "Do you need help? Give me a call. I'll be glad to help out." But then Janet is late for work. The following week she is late again. A pattern begins to emerge. Resentment creeps in. Harmless little questions arise: "Why is Janet late so often? How does she get away with it?"

The office workers don't know that Janet's mother

is sick. Janet is taking her to the doctor in the morning. She has made all the arrangements with her boss, who is allowing her to catch up on her work in the evenings.

When Janet is given a promotion and the others are overlooked, I guarantee you will overhear these three words: *"It's not fair!"*

AT THE AUDITION

Sit in the back of a dark auditorium. Watch as one girl after another takes her place on the bare stage. A tall, thin girl says her name, announces the title of her song, and then proceeds to sing. Her voice is shaky at first, but she grows in confidence and sings well. What you do not see is the endless line of girls waiting backstage for their turn.

They all have waited through the morning. It will be evening before everyone has had a chance to audition. There is only one opening in the cast. One out of over a hundred will be picked. They are all qualified. They have studied, practiced, paid for lessons, worked hard for years and years. For most of these girls this is a life-long dream. It is all they have ever wanted out of life. Yet, only one will be chosen. And the others? They will all cry in their pillow and through their tears you will hear, *"It's not fair!"*

IN THE DOCTOR'S OFFICE

Imagine you are a doctor. Your specialty is Obstetrics/Gynecology. In the course of one day you would see nearly fifty women. Of those women, nearly half would be pregnant. These are women who want their babies. They have carefully planned their pregnancies. They are almost fanatical in their care for their unborn babies. They watch every bite they eat. They consult you before they take any medications. For the next nine months they will question everything they do, see, smell, inhale, or ingest.

There will also be women who will come to see you because they do not want to be pregnant. It was a one-night stand. They can't possibly carry this baby. They don't love the father and certainly don't have room in their lives for a pregnancy. They ask for abortions.

After these women have voiced their anti-baby sentiments, you consult with a woman who has fertility problems. She has tried in vain to get pregnant. Each month she hopes that she will feel the first signs of pregnancy. She longs for a child to hold, a precious baby to cradle in her arms. She cries soft tears. She pleads, "Is there anything you can do for me, Doctor? Is there any hope for me to have a baby?"

Just then the call comes. A pregnancy is terminating too early. A woman is miscarrying and a life is gone. A hope is dashed. Back home a carefully decorated nursery will be closed, with baby clothes packed away. If you were that doctor, I doubt you would be able to get through one day without muttering to yourself, *"It's not fair!"*

IN THE BIBLE

Jesus told the story of the father who had two sons. They worked on his farm and lived well. One day one of his sons came to him with an unusual request, "Hey, Dad, can I have my inheritance early? I mean, if I wait until you're gone, I'll probably be too old to enjoy it."

Dad gives his son his inheritance, so the son takes off. He becomes a real jet-setter. He spends frivolously and lives immorally. Life has become one big party.

Meanwhile big brother stays home and works. He

helps out Dad, keeping him company. He does his work PLUS he does his little brother's work who is off playing around. He consoles himself with the thought that Dad will repay him someday for his loyalty and diligence. He goes so far as to think, "Dad will love me more." But alas, one day he looks down the road to see little brother coming back.

Little brother looks awful. He stinks, while telling how he spent everything. All of his money squandered, he took the only job he could find—feeding pigs. His payment was leftovers from the trough. One day he woke up, looked at himself, and wondered, "Wow! Why am I sticking around here? Why don't I go back home to Dad? He may not take me back, but what have I got to lose?"

Big brother glowers as he listens to his little brother's tale of woes. Surely Dad will remember how hard he worked. Dad will remember all those hot days when he did the work of two sons.

But what does Dad do? He throws open his arms and says to his younger son, "Welcome home! Am I glad to see you! I thought you were gone for good!" Then he turns to his servants and declares, "Bring out the best calf we have. Cook it. Tell everyone that we are going to have a feast! A party! My son who was lost is found!"

Well, I'm sure that if you had a seat by big brother at that party you probably would have heard, *"It's not fair!"*

LIFE'S NOT FAIR . . .

"Life's not fair!" You hear it everywhere—on the playground, the athletic field, in the office, in the entertainment world, in medicine, even in the Bible. As a pastor, I have heard these words more often than I

care to think. Lawyers, spouses, children, students . . . you name it, no one has been immune from the feelings of injustice. Life's unfairness touches everyone at one time or another.

Life's injustices often start at birth. Children aren't born equal. Not at all. I had breakfast the other day with my daughter and her lovely little children. Precious children. And I said, "Life isn't fair. These two kids have everything going for them. A caring father. A devoted mother. A loving home. They grow up in security."

Some children are born into homes ripe with opportunities. Some are nourished with love and encouragement. They have parents who care and provide training, education, materials.

But there are other children who are born to drug addicts. Their mothers are unable to care for them, so they remain the wards of the state. They live in a hospital ward until Mom can undergo treatment or until a foster home can be found. In the meantime, they languish in a plastic cubicle, with no one to hear their cries. Sure, the nurses are there and most of them care, but they are busy. They are overloaded. Their primary function is to provide medical attention. Caressing is not woven into the hospital's budget. These border babies are deprived of love and affection. For too many children, life's injustices start at birth.

For too many, life doesn't get any better with age. You've seen them; so have I, the homeless who push their carts down the street. What's in the carts? All that they own—a few oversized tennis shoes which were probably snatched from a trash can. A tattered blanket. An old, moth-eaten knit cap. Other odds and ends that have seen better days. These pathetic souls search the trash cans for the bitter remnants. They lick the fly-laden styrofoam of melted frozen yogurt cups. They haunt the back doors of restaurants, sleep in parks, and stand on street corners, reminding us that life's not fair!

Fortunately, there are those of us who have been spared these indignities, these abusive blows to our self-esteem. Most of us will never have to try to repair the irreparable damage that these babies and these homeless have endured. Nevertheless, none of us is totally spared insults, injuries, indignities and injustices. We have all experienced rejections. We have all received our share of pink slips, of "No Thank You's." And, regardless of our ages, regardless of our material resources, regardless of our education, race, or social standing, those barbs hurt. They sting; they hit below the belt, and frequently knock the wind out of us. It's hard to believe in a hopeful tomorrow when honest efforts go unrewarded.

I talked to a young student this week. He had applied to a graduate school, this being his second attempt. The first try had resulted in a rejection letter that explained he needed to bring his grade point average up in order to qualify for the program. The letter suggested that he take some more classes, that there would be a good chance for his acceptance to the program if he could maintain a B average. With that encouragement he went to work.

He signed up for classes. He studied. He worked hard. It paid off! The report cards came in with a B+ average! He was sure that the graduate program would accept him now. He reapplied. He waited, watching the mail. Day after day he met the mailman and eagerly searched through the letters and junk mail. Then it came. He recognized the envelope immediately. The results were there, in his hands. All he had to do was to open the letter and then he'd know.

So why was he hesitating? Why was this so hard? Could he take it if they said "No" again? Surely they wouldn't do that. After all, it had been their idea for him to take the "make-up" classes. They had said, "If you have a B average, there'll be no problem." Didn't he have a B average? Better than a B average!

He took the letter and walked nervously up the sidewalk to his home. He tucked the envelope at the back of the pile. He opened the other letters. There was the gas bill, a flyer from a politician. "Oh, yeah, it's almost time to vote." He looked absently at the pennysaver advertising all sorts of used items. *Maybe there's a good buy on a washer and dryer. Our washer and dryer's getting pretty old. It's time to start looking for a replacement,* he thought.

He placed the pile of mail on the kitchen table. The school's envelope was untouched. He had waited so long for his answer. Now, he couldn't face it. He was able to admit to himself, *I'm scared. I don't want to hear bad news.* He looked at the envelope for ten minutes. Ten minutes! Finally, he worked up his nerve and tore open the seal. He slowly unfolded the crisp, embossed paper. He read the verdict, "We're sorry that we will be unable to include you this year . . ."

Rejected!

He said to me, "Dr. Schuller, what do they want from me? *It's just not fair!*"

LIFE'S NOT FAIR!—BUT GOD IS GOOD!

"Really? Is this true? Could it be? Can life be unfair yet God be good?" Yes! Absolutely. But before I show you how, we need to look at some significant questions like:

———

Does this mean that hard work, honest prayer, herculean effort, and relentless possibility thinking does not always pay off? If so—how do we interpret biblical promises like "Ask, and you will receive," (John 16:24), or "Cast your bread upon the waters, for you will find it after many days." (Eccl. 11:1), or "Give, and it will be given to you: good measure, pressed down, shaken together, and running over . . ." (Luke 6:38), or ". . . whatever a man sows, that he will also reap" (Gal. 6:7), or ". . . if you have faith as a mustard seed, you will say to this mountain, 'Move from here to there,' and it will move; and nothing will be impossible for you" (Matt. 17:20)?

Answer: (A) Any strategy for achievement, any philosophy for personal fulfillment, any plan to develop our human potential that ignores work, prayer, effort, and positive thinking will surely fall short of the mark. There can be no argument on that.

(B) The person who seizes opportunities with passion, persistence, and positive attitudes will always be generously and proportionately rewarded. I'm absolutely positive of that!

(C) Beyond a doubt, I am convinced, most of the recorded failures in human development cannot and must not be excused, explained away, and rationalized by "forces out of my control." Again and again and again human beings have achieved the impossible against impossible odds and forces!

Shall we blame such circumstances as poverty, ill health, career stagnation, unemployment, marriage break-ups, destructive addictions, and educational failures on genetics, cultural entrapments, social injustices, power politics, religious or social prejudices (or on Satan—Sin and the Devil)? *All of the above may be sadly, partially true.* But more often than not, such explanations are turned into excuses for personal failures to "Give my dreams all I've got!"

Horrendous obstacles to human achievement do exist enough to allow lethargy, laziness, and despair to take over. Against such self-destructive, negative reactions we need to constantly bombard our minds with motivational power to rise above our circumstances and make our lives great.

(D) Nevertheless—powerful negative forces infect all areas of private and public life. None of us can escape their impact or effect on our lives. People are born with genetic defects. Award winners are not always adequately rewarded. Good people are victims of injustice. Politics can undercut advancements. Sin, greed, and selfishness do brutalize the innocent and the defenseless. Physical fitness devotees die of surprising causes.

Life's not fair . . .
Good things happen to bad people.
Bad things happen to good people.

However, having said all of the above—let this sentence stand: "work out your own salvation with fear and trembling; for it is God who works in you both to will and to do for His good pleasure" (Phil. 2:12–13).

I'm totally convinced that whatever negative realities come our way—in the final analysis, we will be generously vindicated and rewarded if we will "keep the faith" and "keep on keeping on." We may not get what we want—but God will give us what we really need! Our dreams may not always come true—but our hearts' deep, hidden desires shall be fulfilled! "Delight yourself also in the Lord, And He shall give you the desires of your heart" (Ps. 37:4).

My daughter Sheila was in junior high school when she first dreamed of becoming a doctor. She never wavered from that dream. She graduated from Hope College—one of America's best "pre-med" undergraduate schools. But when she applied to medical schools, she was rejected.

She accepted that rejection as a "fact of life"—not an "act of God." She trusted God with her "heart's desire." Today—nearly twenty years and four sons later —she has nearly completed credential studies which will enable her to teach as a public school teacher where she hopes to work as a "doctor" of young minds, bringing mental health through education.

She loves teaching! She has finally discovered her heart's desire! In fact she told me last week, "Dad, I now see that this is what I really wanted to do and be when I first dreamed of becoming a doctor."

I've cried with this girl. I have prayed with this girl, and today she'll tell everybody, "Life's not fair, but God is good."

Don't Confuse the Facts of Life
With
the Acts of God!

Life's not fair: but God is good. And don't get the two mixed up or you'll become a confused atheist or a confirmed agnostic!

"Life" is made up of everything that "happens" to us, or "hits" us. And "life" is the business of living in a sinful world where evil, injustice, and wickedness is very much alive! Place the blame where it belongs: on the facts of life. Not on the acts of God.

The good news is this: *The acts of God can redeem the facts of life.* Keep the faith and God will be with us to guide us through the negative experiences that a negative and sinful—yes, even demonic—world hurls with horrific hurt upon us.

My friend, the world renowned psychiatrist, Victor Frankl, was living in Vienna when Hitler began his persecution of the Jews. He was a young doctor at the time. His parents—fearful and anguished—were thrilled when their son received an invitation to go to America to work. This was his chance to escape the horror on the horizon.

"I was ecstatic," Dr. Frankl told me. "I was already in danger. I was forced to wear the Jewish star exposed like a name tag on a chain—on my chest—for all to see at all times—that I was a Jew. And Jews could not leave the country unless they had a very good reason to emigrate. Armed with my American letter, I walked into the emigration office. As I approached the window, I held my briefcase over my chest—covering my stigmatic sign. I handed the letter to the official and walked out of there with official documents allowing me to leave the country for the freedom and safety of America.

"As I walked back to my office I began to have mixed feelings. Should I abandon my father and mother? Could I—should I—leave them behind? My heart prayed for guidance. When I reached my office I sat, troubled, behind my desk. 'What's this?' I said noticing a broken piece of marble someone had placed in the middle of my desk.

"Just then a colleague came in. 'Look what I found, Dr. Frankl.' He pointed to the marble in my hand. 'I thought you'd like it,' he said, explaining, 'I was walking past the bombed out synagogue and saw this piece. It's the complete capital letter from one of the Ten Commandments! A sign of hope!'

"I asked him which commandment it was from. I'll never forget his reply. His answer was God's answer to my prayer for guidance. He said, 'Honor your father and your mother, that your days may be long upon the land which the Lord your God is giving you' (Ex. 20:12).

"I knew then that whatever the cost, I would not go to America. I tore up my ticket to freedom. I would stay. Yes, I was captured, and sent to a concentration camp. But there I found meaning! And I have survived and lived long! I'm approaching my eightieth birthday!"

Who knows! Had he "acted on his own" instead of "acting on his God," he might have lived a short life in America. Maybe he would have been killed in a car accident! Surely he would never have become what many would say is one of the foremost psychiatrists of the twentieth century.

One is reminded of the Bible verses, ". . . All things work together for good to those who love God, . . ." (Rom. 8:28). ". . . You meant evil against me, but God meant it for good," (see Gen. 50:20) Joseph said to his jealous, conniving brothers who sold him as a slave to a passing caravan of Egyptians. But in Egypt, a prisoner in a foreign and hostile land, he won the favor of the pharaoh and rose to the second most powerful position in that nation. Years later his brothers came to Egypt from their famine-ridden country hopefully to buy grain from this unfriendly, but prosperous government. Imagine their shock when the power man they had to deal with was their long-lost brother whom they had tried to destroy!

Looking into their eyes, Joseph spoke the immortal

words, "You meant it for evil—*But God* meant it for good." He could have said just as well, "I've learned through all these years, *Life's not fair. My family didn't treat me fairly, but God is good!*"

Now I invite you to listen to the testimonies of people who have faced life's unfairness and reacted positively, not negatively, and who gave God a chance to show his goodness.

Gail

I met Gail when her mother brought her to the church where I am a pastor. That was over thirty-five years ago. It was obvious that Gail had been born with Down's Syndrome. Yet, she was never without a smile. She rarely missed a Sunday. And she never failed to brighten the lives of those she touched. But as she got older and got into her twenties she once said to me, "I'll never get married. Nobody will ever love me. I can't even hold down a job. It's not fair."

One day I was talking to her mother. "Mildred, how is Gail doing? She seemed depressed the last time I saw her and that is so unusual for Gail."

"Yes," her mother replied, "She has been discouraged lately. She needs something to give her life meaning. She needs to get her mind off herself."

"Let's look at the possibilities in her life," I suggested. "What can Gail do?"

"I'll tell you one thing about Gail: she can clean. When she cleans the kitchen at home, she cleans corners. She doesn't just wipe, she *rubs* until every spot is off. She polishes the floor and the furniture until it shines."

That gave me an idea. The next Sunday I looked for Gail. I called her over and said, "Gail, I hear you're a good housecleaner."

"Yes," she said, "I'm good. I'm not fast. But I'm good."

"We need someone here in this church who is GOOD!" I answered. "We need clean corners in the church. It doesn't have to be done quickly. But it does need to be done well. If you'd like a job cleaning here at the church, we sure could use you."

She threw up her arms in the air and said, "I'd love it!"

That is how Gail came to work in our custodial department. Everybody loved Gail Bartosh. Her special joy was cleaning the preschool and nursery departments. She had a way with children, and she loved to watch them and keep their areas spotless. It turned out that Gail was handy with a hammer and nails as well. She noticed whenever some of the bookshelves in the preschool needed repair or when sharp corners needed a cushion. She'd invent a soft solution and give the place a safe touch.

We were all concerned and saddened when we learned that they had discovered breast cancer in Gail. She went through the mastectomy. Then they found it in the other breast. Before long it had spread to other parts of her body. She didn't live long. But the days she lived were happy ones. She lived with a mother who loved her child as much as any mother has ever loved any child. Gail worked in a place where she was needed! She was loved.

She said many times to me, "Oh, Dr. Schuller, God is good."

"How do you know, Gail?" I asked.

"Well," she said, "Because of the way you treat me and the way everybody treats me in this church. Everybody here's so nice."

Sharyn

John and Sharyn are the image of success. They work hard, have two fine, teenage sons and more friends than you can count. They are active in their church, in community services, and are valued as neighbors always ready and willing to lend a helping hand. John has been able to make enough money to keep his hobby going, which is restoring old cars. He added an extra garage onto his home to accommodate the tools and the cars undergoing metamorphosis.

By all appearances, John and Sharyn lead a charmed life, except for the fact that John was diagnosed last year as having a rare cancer. Multiple myeloma. Deadly. Extremely painful. The prognosis? One to two years. It's already been one year. Chemo's been rough. Radiation's no picnic. The oncologist has no magic cure.

Life's not fair. It's not fair for John. It's not fair for Sharyn. It's not fair for his sons. Yet, I see his wife from time to time. I ask her how she's doing. Sometimes she cries. Sometimes she laughs. It depends on the day. But always, whether it's with a tear or whether it's with a laugh, she says, "You know, Dr. Schuller. God is so good. God is so good."

"Life's rough, but God's love is enough! His love comes to me through letters, neighbors, friends, and church people!"

I have never ceased to be amazed at how positive people can go through a trial and still smile. They hope while they cope. Of course, they have chosen the wiser route.

Della

I learned a lot about pity, grumbling and complaining from a dear old lady in Orange City, Iowa, when I was visiting my brother, Henry. One afternoon, Henry suggested that we go visit a friend who was in the hospital. While we were there Henry said, "You can't go without saying hello to Della. She's a remarkable old woman. Ninety-two years old. Come meet her, Bob. You'll never forget her."

How right he was! I walked down the sterile hospital hall, and poked my head around the corner, into a hospital room. There, crumpled over, crippled by arthritis, sat a wizened old woman. Her legs were draped by a handmade afghan. She was so still that I thought she might be asleep or even—(well, she didn't look too lively!) Just then, without turning her head, she turned an eye in her socket and gave me a piercing look. Henry responded, "Della, it's me, Henry Schuller. I've come to visit and I've brought a friend for you to meet. It's my brother, Bob. He's the one who preaches on television."

Suddenly her face sparkled with a smile! She said, "Oh, yes! I see him every Sunday morning since I can't get out to church anymore. I don't know what I'd do without him."

She really was one of the most pleasant elderly women I have ever met! She seemed so interested in me. She asked about Henry. Then she asked me to hand her her book.

I looked at the night stand by her chair and noticed a frayed book. There was no title on the book. It looked like a diary. I handed it to her.

"Open it up!"

"Oh, no, I don't want to pry."

"Don't argue! Just do as I say!" she laughed.

I opened the book and saw a myriad of handwritings. This was not a book that she had written in; it was a book that her friends had written in. I saw names. Lots and lots of names, with dates. And in a shaky scrawl next to each name I saw a notation. As I tried to make sense of it all she explained, "This is my prayer book. I pray for everyone who has signed it. You sign it. And I will pray for you."

I did. I never turn down an offer for prayer. I know I need all the help I can get. As I handed the book back to Della, I commented, "There sure are a lot of names in here. Did all these people come to visit you?"

"Oh, yes! I have lots and lots of visitors."

It was obvious to see why Della had so many visitors. She was an absolute delight to be around. As if she could read my mind, she added, "You know I have lots I can complain about. It's not easy to be bound to this chair, all shriveled up. I hate being dependent on others. Sometimes the pain is more than I can bear. But I decided long ago that I wouldn't complain. Who would come visit an old woman if she complained all the time?"

Della knows that God is good. So, she doesn't waste her time saying, "Why me?" Or, "Poor me." Instead she believes that God can help her get through the pain. God has shown her how to be a light who draws people to her room, day after day, year after year.

"Life's not fair . . . but God is good!" This may be impossible for you to say. Especially if you don't believe in God. You are not alone. There are millions of people who don't believe in God. Some of them are very intelligent people. If you are one of those who don't believe in God, you should know that every day you are more alone than you were the day before, for more and more people come to believe in God, and once they experience God, they rarely, if ever turn their back on Him again.

People are discovering God these days in the most

unlikely places. Take the Soviet Union, for example. The leadership of this communist country has done an about face on the subject of faith and the role that it plays in the well-being of a nation. It is no secret that for years, religion was considered an enemy of the state. It was against the law to read the Bible in your home. Believers were persecuted mercilessly. In fact, I came face to face against this opposition to faith, when I agreed to smuggle Bibles into Russia.

Covert Mission

The year was 1968. I had packed the Bibles as instructed. I had agreed to undertake this covert mission because I believed that God's word was direly needed by the people of the Soviet Union. I believed that it was worth risking my safety to deliver God's word to these persecuted believers.

I am not by nature a heroic man. Consequently, I was extremely nervous going through customs in Moscow. My traveling companion, Ike Eichenberger, was also carrying concealed Bibles. He was ahead of me in the customs line. The border guard carefully searched his suitcase. I dared not look at him, for fear that the guards would read the glance of fear. They found nothing. Inwardly I sighed. They hadn't found Ike's Bibles; they probably wouldn't find mine.

Nevertheless, it was with sweaty palms that I handed him my passport. I don't think it was my imagination. He looked at my passport a long time. He read my name and studied my face.

He opened my suitcase and lifted the carefully folded piles of clothing. Suddenly his hand stopped. He pried. He gently prodded. He had discovered my carefully hidden treasure. I had been caught! What would he do to me?

He held up a handful of Bibles and called excitedly to his colleagues. They conversed furtively in Russian. Every now and then they would look in my direction. One of them said in broken English, "You must wait."

After finding my Bibles, they were suspicious of Ike. They recalled his suitcase and a more careful search uncovered his stash as well. I was not naive. I knew that this would not be tolerated. The Bibles were confiscated. We were given a stern warning and then, miracle of miracles, we were allowed to enter the country anyway!

I was overwhelmed by the beauty of this country. I visited every museum I could find. In my search to see and learn as much as I could about the Soviet Union, I heard about the Museum of Atheism in Leningrad. I was shocked but intrigued. I felt that I had to see the museum in order to understand the State's fear of a religious belief system. I called up the guide who had been showing us around. "Have you heard of the Museum of Atheism?"

"Yes, of course!"

"Would you take us to see it?"

"It would be my pleasure."

I had no idea what to expect. Yet I was surprised and saddened to see that the Museum of Atheism was housed in a confiscated Catholic church. This house of God had been transformed into a house of unbelief. The museum hailed proponents of communism and atheists in displays entitled "Heroes of the State." Heroes included such people as Lenin, Castro, and Marx. Our guide enthusiastically told us about each of these men and detailed how they had helped the U.S.S.R.

Then she took us into another room. On the wall were similar profiles, pictures, newspaper clippings, etc. These displays detailed the lives of men and women under the heading "Enemies of the State."

There were pictures of men I knew, like Billy Graham
. . . Martin Luther King . . . the Pope . . . Robert
Schuller . . .

Robert Schuller! I looked again. Sure enough,
there was a picture and a magazine article that told
about my ministry and the unique church I had
founded, a walk-in drive-in church. I blanched. I felt
that same fear that I had felt when the border guards
discovered the Bibles. Our guide looked at my picture,
then she looked at me. Then she looked at the heading
"Enemies of the State."

Without a word, she led us back to our hotel and
left us in the lobby. I was worried. I was in a hostile
country where I had already been caught breaking the
law. Then I was identified in a prominent museum as
an enemy of the State. Ike and I retreated to our
rooms. It felt like the safest thing to do.

That night there was a knock on our door. A man
said simply, "Follow me. Don't ask any questions."

Fear was in Ike's eyes as well as mine as we followed
this mystery man into the night. He put us into the
backseat of a car and drove us through the sleeping
city. We had no idea where he was taking us. Were we
his captives? Were we being taken to a foreign prison?
Would my wife ever know what had happened to me?

We drove silently out of the city and through the
countryside. The trees loomed dark and ominous as
they lined the country roads. The further we got from
civilization, the more concerned I became. Needless to
say, I prayed!

After an hour's drive through the woods of Russia,
we turned onto a side road. Lights shone through the
trees. As we got closer, it became clear that the lights
outlined a runway. A plane stood poised, ready for
take-off. The driver pulled up close to the gangway and
said gruffly, "Get out!"

Another mystery man opened the car door for us, pointed up the gangway to the open door of the plane and said, "Get on!"

We didn't feel that we were in any position to argue, so we did as we were told. Where was this plane headed? What was our destination?

The engine of the plane began to roar. The body of the plane began to rumble. Soon the thrust forced us back into the seat and we soared into the black sky. Without the sun to guide us, it was impossible to know what direction we were going. Was I headed for Siberia? Could we be going West? Could this plane be taking us out of Russia? It seemed like a slim hope, but that one hopeful thought led to another. Of course, they wouldn't risk kidnapping us, holding us here against our will. After all we were citizens of the United States. We had rights. Didn't we?

We flew for hours. Suddenly the plane began to rumble. I had flown enough to recognize the sound of landing gear being lowered into position. We were going to land. But where? The plane tilted downward, tips of trees became visible. Lights, like those of a village shown in the distance. Wherever we were, we were near some semblance of civilization.

It wasn't long before we landed. Hours later I found myself on a train taking me out of Russia to Austria.

Life's Not Fair,
but God Will Have
the Last Word
—and It Will Be Good!

Christmas 1989. The Soviet Union. Twenty years later. My wife and I had been flown into the Soviet

Union by a man who was loved and respected by all Russians. I had been invited to accompany Armand Hammer to the Soviet Union for one purpose—to investigate the possibility of preaching a sermon on the one and only state-controlled television network! Talk about possibility thinking! I found it hard to believe that this was really happening to me. I had returned to the country where I was once branded an enemy of the state, and now was exploring the possibility of preaching to these same people on their state-controlled television network!

Gorbachev had been quoted as saying that the country needed a "faith" if it was going to recover. Armand Hammer felt that I was the person who could open their eyes to the idea of a positive faith. But first, we had to meet with the power people. We had to be interviewed privately, to see if I could meet with their approval.

Armand introduced me to Vladimir Lezutkin. He was *the man* who dictated what is transmitted over the radio and television airwaves. I would have to meet with his approval if I was going to get to address the Russian people. We sat across the table from each other. I was glad that Armand was with me. Lezutkin trusts Armand Hammer. *Will he trust me?* I wondered.

We talked. He asked about our church. He asked what denomination I belonged to. Am I Catholic? Am I Muslim? Am I Protestant? Yes? Lutheran? Methodist? When I replied that I belonged to the Reformed Church in America, he responded, "Wonderful! The Reformed Church is well known and well respected in Europe and East Europe."

He told me what his needs were. "We must not offend anyone. The person who talks on Russian television will be talking to all faiths at once—Russian Orthodox, Catholic, Jewish, Muslim, Protestant. Can you deliver a message that would not offend the people who belong to another faith?''

"Yes."

"Our people are full of despair. They need someone to give them hope. Can you deliver a message that will bring hope?''

"Yes. People everywhere are the same. We share universal needs—the need for faith, hope, and love."

The interview continued. Lezutkin asked several more questions. Finally he stood up and said, "I think you are the man to speak to the people of the Soviet Union. You have good things to say. Let us see what we can arrange. You know, you would be the first foreigner in history to be allowed to preach on Soviet television."

He leaned across the table and shook my hand. As his strong hand grasped mine, he said, "I must tell you something, Dr. Schuller. I will let you talk about God on television, but I don't believe in Him. After all, I have never experienced God."

I looked this strong man in the eyes and said, "Oh! But you have! You have experienced God—many times —*you just didn't recognize Him.* That time when you felt love for your wife or your daughter . . . That time when you held back a tear because you were touched by an emotion that seemed to come from seemingly nowhere—that was God. You just didn't call it by the right name."

Lezutkin's eyes glistened for just a moment. He pulled away and said, "I will be in touch as soon as we are able to arrange a studio."

I was asked to "wait outside." We were both excited about the opportunity to speak to the Russian people, but I was nervous. What would I say? Would they want to screen my message ahead of time? I had heard how strictly the television was controlled. It was common

practice for all scripts to be submitted ahead of time
for censorship purposes. How would my message be
handled?

Just then the call came. I was to report immediately
to a television studio down the hall. I was quickly
ushered to the studio where I was met by a well-known
Soviet reporter. We chatted briefly. Then she said, "We
have decided that we will do a short interview with you.
Then I will turn the platform over to you. You will have
ten to fifteen minutes to address the Soviet people. Are
you ready?"

Now! Right now? Surely, she meant we would do
this tomorrow. Not now? Not today! I looked around,
there was the director, cameramen were adjusting their
cameras, the lights were being turned on, an audio
technician began clamping a microphone on my tie, I
gulped, "Sure! I'm ready!" But inside I screamed,
"What am I going to say? Lord, help me!"

Lights. Camera. Action: The pretty young television
reporter turned to the camera and began her introduction. It was in Russian, but the interpreter translated
instantly into the earphone I was wearing. I heard her
say, "Good evening. We start today's program in a
rather unusual manner. It will be a very different program. For the first time in the history of Soviet television we have invited a foreigner to come to our Russian
television and preach a sermon about God! Today we
have a rather unusual guest. On his most recent trip to
the Soviet Union, Dr. Hammer, the famous American
businessman, invited Pastor Schuller to come with him.
Pastor Schuller is a preacher with the Reformed
Church in California. He is very well known to Americans, because he delivers sermons on television every
week. Dr. Schuller, where did the idea of televising a
sermon in America come from?"

Fortunately my reply was taped. Otherwise I never

would have been able to tell you how I answered Natalia. You see, I was so nervous that the entire half hour was a blank in my memory bank. Listening later to the tape, I heard myself answer, "Well, I started a brand new church with my wife—just the two of us, and it grew faster and faster. We built a church that could hold 1500 people but after ten years we had outgrown it. There just wasn't room for all of the people. So we started televising the services. That way, people who could not get out to go to church could see it in their homes or in their hospital rooms."

Next question: "What was your sermon based on? What is the most important element for you?"

I said, "One concept. Call it encouragement. Hope. Self-confidence and enthusiasm for life. Everything we do in our ministry, in our messages, in our music, in our architecture, is to restore balance to people's lives. I can live without pleasure, but I can't live in shame. People cannot humiliate me; they cannot strip me of my pride, unless I allow them to. I have a life and I'm proud of who I am. And that's true for every living human being. And that is the essence of what religion's all about—finding and restoring people's hurt pride."

Natalia then asked, "When you are preaching your sermon, do you intend it only for believers, or do you address it to the entire American people, and now to the whole world, to believers and nonbelievers?"

"That's a wonderful question." I replied, "It's why I'm different from many preachers and rabbis. I'm primarily interested in talking to people who don't have religion. People who have religion can go to the church, temple, or mosque."

"I see," said Natalia. "And tell me, do you think— and if so, why?—that both nonbelievers and believers all over the world need this sermon?"

"I think that all human beings need affirmation

and encouragement. Every single person every day meets some disappointment. And we can't allow that disappointment to grow into discouragement. So, I think everybody needs hope—everybody needs enthusiasm—and everybody, every day, needs to have their spirit lifted. This is the goal of a Christian service, to help people feel excited and happy with who they are."

Next question: "Dr. Schuller, you are here. Are you convinced that our people will understand what you have to say to them?"

"Oh, yes. Because I know people, and people are the same all over the world. They have dreams; they have hurts; they have memories—some good memories and some bad memories. They like babies. They like love. All human beings are the same. That's my specialty. And the Bible, God, and Jesus Christ tell me how I can treat people beautifully. Yes, they will understand my message."

Then Natalia did a remarkable thing. She turned to me and said, "Then I will leave you and the Soviet people alone together. Please go ahead. Talk to them from your heart."

I gulped. I had no time to think for the red light of the camera was on. Every moment was being recorded. I had been given the opportunity to talk to the Soviet people, uncensored. But I'd had no time to prepare my thoughts. I had to speak now—the only problem was—what was I going to say? I prayed and believed that the God Who had given me the gift of speech would not fail me now. This is what I said:

"I cannot begin to thank you for this wonderful honor. I would like to share some thoughts with you, my brothers and sisters in the Soviet Union. It's Christmas time, and Christmas is when we remember the words of Jesus: 'Peace I give to you.'

Don't Confuse The . . .
FACTS OF LIFE

With The
ACTS OF GOD!

"I'm so excited, because Christmas 1989 marks the first time in the United States of America that we really trust the Russian people.

"I have a confession to make: There has been a great deal of distrust between our countries; at least we have been guilty of it. There was a great distrust—until something happened—and I can tell you the day that it happened: December 3, 1989.

"My friend, President George Bush, met with your President, Mikhail Gorbachev. They sat together, shoulder to shoulder, in a live, globally televised news conference. When the American people saw that, there was a birth of trust on a level I have never experienced or known.

"And so I can say to you that the American people trust the Russian people, and that's so beautiful because trust sets the stage for real love. Real love, comraderie, harmony, peace are never possible between two persons or between two countries, unless first there's trust.

"So we're ready to step into a new decade. The 1990s, I predict, will be a decade of peace. The new millennium will soon come, and we will all—in the Soviet Union and in America—look forward to each day, each tomorrow without fear.

"So I have a special gift for you—a very beautiful gift. It is a promise, a prophecy from the Bible. In the Old Testament, in Jeremiah 29:11, God speaks: 'For I know the thoughts that I think toward you,' says the Lord, 'thoughts of peace and not of evil, to give you a future and a hope.'

"Never have we been able to look forward to tomorrow with such hopefulness, such optimism. Think of it—the wars that people were afraid might come, will never come. The nuclear bombs are all going to be dismantled. War is obsolete. We will all live together in peace, not just in the next decade but forevermore.

"Think of it: Many people are still dying from cancer. But my dear friend, Dr. Armand Hammer, just last year was raising millions of dollars in America to find a cure for cancer. We are making progress. I predict by the year 2000 most cancers will be cured.

"We stand on the edge of a wonderful time in history. Television programs are broadcast from Russia to America and from America to the Soviet Union. With satellites in the sky, we are able to talk to each other, understand each other, care about each other, give hope to each other, love each other—that's our tomorrow.

"Now, you say to me, 'Prove to me that there is a God.' And I say, 'When so much good is happening, you prove to me that there is no God.' You say, 'What is God?' And I say, 'He is not flesh and bones, but rather He is a Spirit.'

"And how can you experience Him? Why, you experience Him when an idea comes to your mind. Where does the idea come from? It's a creative idea; it's a wonderful idea. Maybe the idea can become a song. Maybe the idea can become an invention. Maybe the idea can become a breakthrough in negotiations so that people who are hostile become friendly.

"I have four daughters, one son, and twelve grandchildren. When we have get-togethers, there are twenty-four of us around the table—all ages. A wonderful family. But our family has had some tough times.

"My wife had cancer and had a breast removed. The toughest time was when I was in Korea. I was ministering and I got a telephone call. The call was from an American and the caller said, 'Dr. Schuller, your daughter Carol has been in a terrible accident.' Carol was thirteen at the time. I wish I had a picture of her.

She's as beautiful as the Russian children I've seen here.

"She went for a ride as a passenger on a motorcycle. Her driver went faster and faster. All of a sudden, he hit an oncoming car, and Carol was thrown through the air seventy-five feet. Her left leg was hanging by a tendon. She was bleeding badly and screaming in pain.

"The doctor came, but couldn't give her anything for her pain. So she endured the pain as she was rushed to the hospital. The doctor worked to save her life. She had blood transfusions—seventeen pints of blood. Now, that is getting pretty close to losing your life. The doctor called me in Korea and said, 'We are going to have to amputate her leg.' The word cut through me like a knife—*amputate!* My wife and I caught the first plane home to America.

"On the way back, I could tell I was going to cry. I went to the toilet and closed the door. I started to cry out loud, and I prayed, 'Oh God, if there is a God, why did this have to happen?' It hurt me so badly to know when I got home my daughter would have only one leg. Then a thought went through my mind: *Play it down, and pray it up.* I thought to myself, *It's not so bad. She still has one leg, two arms, her face, two eyes—she's alive! Look at what she has left, instead of what she has lost.*

"Today, twelve years later, that beautiful girl is married and has two little children. She is very happy. Do you know what she would say if she were here today? She would say what I said earlier, from the Bible: 'I have a plan for your life, a plan for good, not evil, a plan to give you a future with hope.'

"You can choose either to be a skeptic or a believer. Birds were meant to fly. Flowers were meant to bloom. Humans were designed to believe in beauty, in love, in truth, in God.

"My friends, thank you. Have a blessed and prosperous New Year. In 1990 you and I will become friends. America and Russia will help each other. We are comrades.

"I don't understand or speak Russian, but I have a famous American saying, and I want to see if I can say it in Russian:

"Se Vami Lubov Boga E Moia Tozhe!"

"In English, it's 'God loves you, and so do I.' "

"Se Vami Lubov Boga E Moia Tozhe!"

That entire message aired just that way across the Soviet Union on Christmas Day 1989. I received this telegram from Lezutkin, "Over two hundred million people heard your message!" Five months later I was invited to have lunch with Mikhail Gorbachev in Washington, D.C. "Your message calmed our nation," he announced to me and to the international press gathered in the Russian Embassy. As this book goes to press, I have already delivered three sermons over the entire Russian television network.

Amazing, isn't it? An entire nation that has worked for over seventy years to eradicate faith in God has done an about-face. Today the Soviet people have come to the realization that life is empty, life is bleak, life is hopeless without faith in God. They are looking for God. They are eagerly searching for a vital faith. They are learning that life's not fair but GOD IS GOOD! God will have the last word.

"After seventy years of atheism we have discovered," Lezutkin said to me, "that there are positive human emotions that only come through the religious channel!"

Does God exist? Is He good? Open your mind to the incredible possibility! After all, if one entire country can open its mind to the possibility that faith is the only answer and the only hope, then maybe you can open your mind to this creative concept as well. Take a look around you. More people believe in a good God everyday. Maybe you should too.

Just because you don't believe in God, doesn't mean He's not working with you. You may call it a mood shift. You may have thought that you just got a bright idea. You didn't recognize it was the presence of an inner spirit that the Bible calls God. You thought, *What a lucky break.* You didn't realize it was God! How do you recognize God? Be alert to Him! Give Him a chance to come into your life.

I don't know what it is you're facing. I don't know why you bought this book, or why someone gave it to you. One thing I do know—life's not fair but God is alive! Have you been dealt a rotten deal? Are you overwhelmed, even thinking of calling it quits for good?

Hang in there! Give faith a chance! There is a new beginning for you waiting to be discovered. Take one tiny step right here and right now. Open your heart. Just a little bit. Be brave enough to think, *Maybe there is a God. Maybe He does love me. Maybe He will get me through this. Maybe, just maybe, I'll begin to dream again.*

CHAPTER TWO

The Game of BLAME and SHAME

A TALE OF TWO BROTHERS

The house reeked of stale alcohol. The dim light filtered through thick, hazy air. Flies hovered over piles of dirty dishes. Despair hung heavy in the room. Dad was sacked out on the thread-bare couch.

Two brothers sat at the cluttered kitchen table. One was reading his school book diligently, the other was toying with his food, scanning the *T.V. Guide.* One father, two boys. One situation—an alcoholic father, an absent mother. Both boys lived with the same verbal and physical abuse, neglect, and despair.

One brother ran with friends who helped him in his search for an escape. Like his father, he found it in drugs and alcohol. This second-generation alcoholic lived from glass to glass, finding odd jobs, earning just enough money to keep bottles in the house.

The second brother lost himself in school work. Teachers praised his efforts. Starving for affection and attention, the lad excelled. He lapped up the positive reinforcement. He worked hard and won a scholarship to a noteworthy academy. He went on to become a well-known, respected lawyer.

One day the newspaper chose to do a profile of their local hero. The reporter asked the esteemed citizen, "Is it true that your father was an alcoholic?"

"It's true. I had an alcoholic father—that's why I am where I am today. I decided early on I wasn't going to waste my life the way he did!"

Meanwhile, the first brother continued in his drunken path of destruction until the day a kind-hearted employer intervened. He was given the choice of losing his job or entering a rehabilitation program. He chose the latter.

The counselor in the rehab center listened as the boy described his childhood. He shook his head sadly as the broken young man recalled a much-too-familiar scene of alcoholic behavior. He heard words too familiar to him: "I had an alcoholic father—that's why I am where I am today."

One home. One father. Two brothers. Two different reactions. Why? What accounts for two opposite forces—one positive, one negative; one constructive, one destructive?

There are a variety of factors that, when mixed together, result in a personality and a temperament and a frame of mind that reacts to adversity either positively or negatively. We are born with a certain personality type, we come into the world with definite temperaments. There are several interesting books and philosophies that deal solely with the interpretation and analysis of personalities. Some employers give personality tests. Marriage counselors give temperament tests.

These tests, when properly administered and interpreted can be an important step toward understanding ourselves. However, they are simply a first step. They are not an end. We are creatures of choice and we have the ability to choose how we will react to any circumstance. We are creatures of great adaptability and therefore we have the freedom to alter, adjust to, or abdicate our circumstances.

Once we understand who we are and why we are the way we are, then we need to look at where we are, where we want to go and how we will get there. That, I suggest, is what the one brother did. He looked at who he was—the son of an alcoholic. Then he looked at where he wanted to go—anywhere different from where he was. Then he asked himself, *How will I get there?* The path to freedom for him was through school.

If you said to this young man, "Life wasn't fair to you." He would probably agree. He would also add, if you asked him, "And I didn't deserve the bad father I had." Then a miracle happened. He discovered his real value as a person.

His teachers opened his eyes to the fact that he was a wonderful human being, that he deserved the best, not the worst. He deserved the best home in the county. He deserved the best father in the state. He deserved far more love and affection than he got. So his self-esteem was redeemed by teachers who helped him see that "Life wasn't fair—and he DIDN'T deserve it!" Furthermore he had to make his life good and great—life wouldn't hand it to him.

On the other hand, the brother who followed in Dad's footsteps fell into that deathly trap of negative thinking.

He was destroyed by thoughts such as, *I got what I deserved. I am a bad boy, so I got a bad home. I am bad, so I got a father who beats me. I deserve every whipping I got. I deserve every derisive comment Dad made.*

Those comments reflect a shattered self-esteem and

illustrate how vulnerable this boy was. It is no wonder that he never even tried to amount to anything.

These two brothers symbolize the human race. We all react to life's injustices in one of two ways. We either say, "Life's not fair—and I DO deserve it! I'll just have to accept it." Or we say, "Life's not fair—and I DON'T deserve it! So I'll make my life great!"

THE GAME OF SHAME

Shame! We've all experienced it, some more than others. Unfortunately, some people jump to the conclusion that when things go wrong it is because of something they have done wrong. They have gotten what they deserve. They think little of themselves, suffer from a low self-esteem, and berate themselves for their failures. For these people, shame is a primary reaction to life's problems.

A husband leaves. The wife left behind thinks, *I was not a good enough wife. If I had kept the bathrooms cleaner, if I had spent less time reading and more time talking to him, maybe he wouldn't have left.* The list is endless. She feels worthless. Her sense of shame festers like a boil drawing the strength she could devote to putting her life back together.

A business goes bankrupt. The papers are signed; the equipment is put on the block; the notices are mailed; shop is closed. And what do some of these bankrupt businessmen feel? "It's my fault. I am a failure! If only I had worked harder, if only I had been more diligent."

Searing, debilitating, life-threatening shame. What is it? *Shame is blame turned inward.* The persons who suffer from feelings of shame blame themselves. You will hear this phrase often in their language, "It's my fault."

People who suffer from shame are quick to think, "Life's not fair and I DO deserve it!"

THE SABOTAGE SYNDROME

What do you deserve?

You deserve to be a success. Yes, you do! And if you have trouble believing that, then you need to work on your self-esteem. For the truth of the matter is, that if you suffer from a low self-esteem, you will never feel successful. Even if, by some chance, you do find happiness or success, if you suffer from low self-esteem, you will end up losing the happiness that you have stumbled upon.

People who don't believe that they deserve to be successful, will sabotage the good that is happening in their lives. They will drive away the husband that is good to them; they will push away the child who loves them; they will antagonize the boss that believes in them; they will over-extend their line of credit, and end up losing it all. Why? Because they don't believe they deserve it.

Life's not fair. But is this what you deserve? It is imperative that you ask yourself this question and come up with a satisfactory answer, because it is the root of getting you successfully through any tragedy. It is also the foundation for building a new beginning.

The first question I hear from people when they get hurt is, "Why me?" But that's the wrong question. It can produce self-doubt and even self-contempt. The right question to ask is, Why not you? This question recognizes that *what happens to you is incidental to who you are*. Tragedies happen because tragedies are part of life. Death is part of life. You cannot have life without death, and you cannot have happiness without sadness. You cannot have life without hurts.

Diane Fraley is one of the most beloved teachers in the school where my grandson, Jason, attends. Jason stopped off at her classroom every afternoon for a chat and a piece of candy from her well-stocked candy jar. But he became bitterly disappointed when he learned that she wouldn't be his teacher anymore. He continued, however, to stop off and visit with her after school and in the process became good friends with her son, Brad, who is also ten years old.

Little did either of the boys know that Diane was going for radiation every morning before school and chemotherapy every weekend. Neither boy noticed that she was wearing a wig to cover up the thinning hair. All they saw was her warmth and the welcome she extended to them whenever they stopped by. They only saw a mother who was just as involved as always. They worked at her kitchen table together on their fourth grade report, using the books that Diane had checked out for them at the library.

It was only when the time came for Diane to go to the hospital for a special bone marrow treatment that the boys had any inkling anything was wrong. The news that their beloved friend and mother was sick and going to the hospital for a month in isolation came as a shock to these boys. Naturally, they were scared. This teacher and mother that they loved was threatened. The children in her classroom were equally upset. They could hardly talk about it without crying.

When Jason heard the news he rushed home to his mother. "Mrs. Fraley's in the hospital!"

"What's wrong?"

"She has cancer. She has tubes coming out of her where they feed her strong medicines. She'll be in the hospital for a month. Will she be O.K.?"

"I'm sure the doctors are doing everything they can. I'll find out what we can do to help."

Jason's mother called Diane. She found out that Diane had a reoccurrence of breast cancer. The prognosis was grim. Her only hope was a bone marrow treatment. The plan was to harvest Diane's own marrow, treat it and kill off the cancer cells and then transplant the cleansed marrow back into Diane's system. There, the clean cells would multiply and heal her. If it worked, the doctors would call it a "cure." The risk was great. She would be taken to the brink of death, a point at which her immune system would be void of any protective measures. There would be no white blood cells to fight off any infections. She would be as vulnerable as any human being could be.

Consequently, she would be in a special isolation unit until the bone marrow started manufacturing white blood cells again. She would be able to see her family in her hospital room, provided they had adequately scrubbed up, wore masks and gowns and were sure they carried no infectious disease. She would be in that one room for one month, provided all went well.

Diane said good-bye early to her class. They had a substitute for the last month of school.

The treatment had horrendous side effects. Worst of all was the separation from her family. It meant that she missed her oldest son's high school graduation. That was a bleak week. But it worked! The new, healthy marrow kicked in and started producing a bountiful harvest of white blood cells. Today she's back at home. She's back in the classroom. Jason and Brad would like to stop for candy after school, but they have moved up to middle school. Life goes on. There are no guarantees, no promises that we will be spared from hurt and pain—no matter how good we may be.

There's no question that Diane deserves to live! Everyone deserves a healthy, happy life. Unfortunately, living a good life, doing all the right things, heeding all the right warnings, will not guarantee that life will be free of sickness or death. We can only do the best we can, take what life deals to us, and believe that we deserve the best!

YOU deserve the best! You deserve to get well. You deserve to succeed. You deserve to have happy, fulfilling relationships.

And when you don't get what you deserve then admit it, "I'm O.K. But life's not fair! Life's not fair, but God is good—anyway!"

Don't fall victim to the misconception that good rewards always follow good behavior and bad punishments always follow bad behavior.

If you are the kind of person who plays the game of shame when you run into an injustice, if you automatically think it's your fault, then you probably need to work on building up your self-esteem. Even those of us with a healthy self-esteem suffer a confidence blow out from time to time.

I have discussed the subject of self-esteem in many previous books, and if you think you need to boost up your self-esteem, you could try reading one of those books in addition to this one. Before you do, try these:

SELF-ESTEEM BOOSTERS

#1. Give Yourself a Pat on the Back.

If you are whipping yourself, trade in the whip for a pat. Instead of self-flagellation, try self-congratulations. Yes! Even if the business has folded, even if the escrow fell through, even if the relationship came to a screeching halt, you deserve a pat on the back.

It's true—you made mistakes. Yes, you probably could have worked harder. And you were perhaps a little naive and too trusting. There were things that you did wrong. But there were things you did right! Yes, there were! And it's time you began to look at them and take account of them.

Look at your mistakes and learn from them. Look at your correct answers and remember them. The next time you are tested, you may be surprised how much higher your score will be.

You may think you have failed, but in reality, it could be that you were spared from something. You weren't accepted into the program, but is it really what YOU want? You didn't get the job, but was the job really right for you? You didn't get the proposal, but was the guy really right for you? Maybe we can all learn and identify with Janice. Here's her story:

Janice pulled back the plastic cover to admire her gown one more time. She lovingly caressed the satin folds and fingered the delicate beads that outlined the bodice. She picked up the veil and arranged it on her head. She imagined how lovely her wedding day would be.

She picked up her checklist, even though she knew it by heart. Everything had been done long before. The flowers had been chosen, the cake was ordered. The music arrangements had been made. The final count had been called in to the caterer. In only three more days her dream would come true. She would walk down the aisle and begin her new life committed to the man she loved.

She was putting away the list when the phone rang. Her mother called up the stairs. It was John. *Is he as nervous as I am?* she wondered with a laugh as she bounded down the stairs. "Hi, John! How are you?"

"Not good."

His voice sounded so flat, so unlike the cheery young man she had grown to love. Immediately her protective instincts told her something was dreadfully wrong. She pushed back the fears that leaped to her mind. "What's wrong?"

"I don't know."

His silence engulfed her. Tears sprang to her eyes. She gulped them back. "Well, why did you call?"

"I can't go through with it."

Her head reeled. Her knees got weak. Had someone hit her in the stomach? No? Then why did she feel as though she had just had the wind knocked out of her?

Maybe she had heard wrong. "Can't go through with what?"

"The wedding. I can't go through with the wedding. I'm sorry."

Click. He was gone. Nothing left but a dial tone. She never heard from him again.

Her father came to see me, as I was supposed to be the officiating minister at the wedding. This was not the first time I had seen a last-minute cancellation of a wedding. Brides and grooms are left waiting at the altar more often these days. Naturally they are bitterly disappointed. I can't think of a more fatal blow to a person's self-esteem than to be publicly rejected and humiliated in this way. It isn't fair! No one deserves to be treated like that! Yet it happens. And more often than not the waiting bride or groom bears a tremendous burden of self-imposed blame.

Janice included. She blamed herself. She assumed that John backed out of the wedding because she did something she shouldn't have done or she gave less than he needed from her. She nearly drove herself crazy trying to figure out what she had done wrong.

In reality, I doubt that Janice did anything wrong. Janice is a lovely young woman. She is talented, intelligent, responsible, warm, caring. Any man would have been proud to have been her groom. Janice needed to open her eyes to all the good that she was. She needed to recognize that John was the one who had a problem. And as hurt as she was, she was probably spared even more hurt, for marriage to a man who is afraid of commitment can be a lifetime of loneliness.

I met with Janice and her father. I told her she did not deserve to be hurt. John had not treated her right. Her tears were a natural reaction. But I pointed out to her that her hurt was turned inward. Her critical self-examination, her game of self-blame would destroy her. This incident could be just the end of a relationship with a man of dubious integrity, or it could be the destruction of her self-esteem.

I encouraged her to pamper her bruised pride. Like any other wound, it needed to be treated with loving care. I prescribed heavy doses of self-affirmation. I encouraged her to write a list of all that she liked about herself. I cautioned her against her self-flagellations and advised substituting beatings with pats on the back.

Are you disappointed with what life has handed you? Do you blame yourself for your tragedy? Are you beating yourself needlessly? If so, STOP!

Give yourself a pat on the back. Affirm yourself, and accept compliments from others who are trying to comfort you. Yes, be honest, there are people who have been kind and have offered their support. You have not believed them? You have brushed aside their encouragements? Why?

Sometimes we would rather wallow in our self-pity and push away love, afraid to believe the good that we hear. We are too quick to believe the bad that others say about us, and too quick to reject the affirmations of loving friends. Be good to yourself. Accept the praise. Believe in yourself—others do!

#2. *Look At What You Have Left; Don't Look At What You've Lost.*

Sound trite? Have you heard this saying before? You have? Well, have you applied it lately?

"Easier said than done. You don't know what I've lost, Dr. Schuller."

True. I don't know what you have lost but I know that it has dealt a deathly blow to your self-esteem or you wouldn't be reading this book. Your self-esteem has been damaged. It probably needs to be admitted to Intensive Care.

You're hurting. That's O.K. But the sooner you begin treatment, the sooner you will get well. Begin by looking at this from a positive point of view. Begin by applying this time-approved saying. The phrase is trite, I'll admit. But it still gets my vote. Why? Because it works.

You say, "But, Dr. Schuller, what have I got left?"

You have one precious commodity that no one can ever take from you. *You have the freedom to choose what you will do now, where you will go from here, and how you will react to this blow.*

You can choose to be bitter. You can choose to slide into a deep pit of self-pity, or you can choose to react positively. You can look at this setback as an opportunity for learning for growth, painful as it may be. What happens to you IS important, but it is not the end. You have the ability to write a happy ending. You have the freedom to choose a positive reaction and, believe me, a positive reaction is always the best way to go!

If you ever attend the Crystal Cathedral, watch out for Gary Franken. Gary never misses a Sunday and he always has a smile ready for anybody who will receive it. The regular churchgoers all know Gary and they are quick to return his sunny greeting, but visitors are more reticent. They do not know Gary and are uncomfortable with his appearance. You see, Gary has cerebral palsy. He has limited control over his muscles, including his legs, his arms, and the muscles that control speech; therefore, his language is hard to understand.

That never stops Gary. He is always quick to strike up a conversation. He has so much to say—and what he has to say is certainly worth listening to. Unfortunately, in our society, people are too busy to take the time to listen to Gary's words. Those who do never forget them.

Gary has beaten the odds. When he was born with the umbilical cord wrapped around his neck, the doctors predicted that he would never walk. The prognosis was grim. The experts pointed out every ability that had been taken away from Gary. But Gary, with the help of his family, refused to accept the dark side of the picture. He insisted on focusing on what he had left and how he could multiply it.

So he learned to walk. Then he learned to drive. Gary says that the hardest part was finding a teacher who would dare to teach him. He developed his brilliant mind, so that today he works for Cal-Trans, the California State Department of Transportation. He is the Associate Transportation Planner, working in the area of planning improvements in transportation in California, whether it would be for more freeways or for better public transportation. Currently, he is working in System Planning which is long range planning. He also serves as chair and vice-chair on committees that require him to travel up to Sacramento.

Wow! If you live or have driven in California, you have a tiny glimpse of how complicated and difficult this task must be. You can appreciate the mind that is locked in a body, an outward shell that inhibits people from getting to know this precious soul. For day after day Gary endures prejudice. He has been snubbed, ignored, and mistreated because of his handicap.

Once I asked Gary about it. He said, "I think it is really unfair that some people do not perceive my space suit, meaning my physical exterior, as just a different type of vehicle that carries both my mind and my soul. I wish there was a way that prejudgment could be eliminated from this world. The saddest part is that some people who see me and talk to me for the first time, have a tendency to relate my condition to mental retardation.

"I have to relate everything to reality because having cerebral palsy, there is no room for idealism or fantasy. I need to be willing to ignore what people do not understand about me and just focus on what I believe I must do in order for my life to be fulfilling to myself."

I said, "Gary, do you think people expected for you to come as far as you have?"

"No, I guess that some people focus on the handicap rather than on the person that is inside the handicap, which is another way of saying that they put boundaries around someone else's life. I always keep reminding myself of one very important element in life, and that is if I choose to let others plan my life for me, then I am giving God an opportunity to fail at His own creation. But if I am willing to take responsibility for my handicap and be willing not to walk away from it by feeling sorry for myself, then I believe that I am giving God an opportunity to succeed with my life."

I could not pass up the opportunity to probe deeper. I wanted to know what this remarkable man thought of God. He had every right to be bitter. He had suffered unfair humiliation, prejudice, and discrimination. I said to him, "You mention life's unfairness. You mention God. How do the two fit together?"

"Well, I believe that there is a God and that He sees everything that I do in life. I think of all the disappointments, of all the teardrops, of all the laughter, and if I did not believe that there is a God who is watching everything that I do, then I don't think I could have made it this far because there were so many times that I wanted to give up. But I knew that if I did that, then everything that I worked for and accomplished would have been for nothing. I always keep in mind that life can be treated as stepping stones which brings me that much closer to the real purpose of life. And to me the real purpose to life is being able to say to myself, 'Gary, you have done the best you could with what you were given to work with.' I think that if everybody can say that, then this world would be very dynamic to live in."

Wise words for all of us: HAVE YOU DONE THE BEST WITH WHAT YOU WERE GIVEN TO WORK WITH?

Most of us have so much left that we've neglected to do anything with. Be positive. Be realistic. There is always much more LEFT that we can do something positive with.

#3. Re-evaluate Your Assets.

In time of stress, it's easy to overlook hidden assets. We all have resources that we neglect and forget. Economists are familiar with the term "dead assets". Those are assets that have been lying in a drawer, a bank vault or in an envelope, and you've forgotten them. You have material assets that you have not taken into consideration.

Likewise, you have emotional and spiritual strengths that you have ignored. You may have neglected them because you haven't needed them. Now is the time to discover just how strong your faith really is. The good news is that most everybody I talk to in time of stress tells me how strong their faith was. They didn't realize how much faith they had until they needed it.

One of my favorite pieces of music is the well-known Ninth Symphony by Beethoven. The theme from this symphony was adopted as a hymn tune—"Joyful, Joyful." It is also the opening theme for the Hour of Power.

Leonard Bernstein gave a parting gift to the world the last year of his life when he conducted a historical rendition of this symphony in celebration of the fall of the Berlin wall. It was a moving sight to see the combined orchestra and chorus of East and West Germans singing together, *"Friede, friede . . ."*

Of course, that is a Germanic play on words that Bernstein incorporated to celebrate the moment. Beethoven's original score reads, *"Freude, freude . . ."*

The difference? Beethoven's translates "Joyful, joyful." Bernstein's translates "Peace, peace."

I watched Bernstein and his historical assembly of musicians and was moved as was the rest of the world. I could not help but remember the story of the original performance of the Ninth Symphony.

Beethoven was at his zenith, a well-known, respected, loved composer in Vienna. Then, tragedy of tragedies. His hearing began to go. A degenerative disease destroyed his hearing until he was totally deaf. He could not hear a sound.

Unfair? Of course! Of all people to be denied hearing, Beethoven would have been the last. Not only was the loss his, it was also a loss for all of humanity, for never again would he be able to produce and create glorious music.

At least that is how it appeared to all of Vienna when he left the music world. He retreated to a monastery where he could be alone with his private pain. While he was there, God spoke to him. He gave him music that Beethoven alone could hear in his mind. The music was glorious.

Writing furiously, Beethoven's brilliant talent translated silent sounds to marks on paper that could be read and performed by musicians. The results were phenomenal. And music historians all know the story of Beethoven's great comeback. He stood next to a conductor. He faced the great chorus and the symphony in the beautiful hall of Vienna with the audience seated behind him.

The strings played the soft, sensitive first movement of the symphony. Beethoven followed along with his score. In his mind he could "hear" the entire performance. He could "hear" the passage when the woodwinds entered and then the brass instruments. The music swelled and ebbed, ever building until the bass vocalist added his rich notes, bringing in the other soloists and finally the full chorus. Instruments and singers combined sang out in joyful jubilation, "Joyful, joyful!"

What a comeback it was! The audience leaped to its feet in thunderous applause. Because Beethoven could not hear the applause, the conductor turned him to face the adulation of the audience. It was a spectacular moment in music history. And even today we sing and re-sing Beethoven's testimony, "Joyful, joyful!"

Who would have thought that anyone was capable of creating his best music *after* losing his hearing? Would Beethoven have realized the depth of his faith had he not gone deaf? No one knows for sure. This we do know: *There are vast untapped resources of faith and talent that can be discovered only in adversity.*

#4. *Pump Up Your Possibility Thinking:*

When disappointments hit, it's time to pump up your possibility thinking with such affirmations as:

- "I still have great possibilities left."
- "I can begin again."
- "I can retreat" (there's nothing wrong with that; regroup, reorganize, revise plans, and then move ahead again.)
- "This is just a bend in the road; it's not the end of the road."

When disappointments hit, it's time to square your chin and make some positive decisions. Things have changed. Life's different. You're facing a new direction. Looking at the road map of your life, where do you want to end up? You have the choice to go wherever you want to go. There are many ways of getting there.

Begin by believing in God. Believe in His future for you. You can make it! God will give you the dream if you will ask Him and He will provide the resources if you will look to Him.

I can't think of anything more exciting than change. We live in a world where most people are not locked into their circumstances. Walls are falling; airwaves are being freed up; restrictions are being lifted. Hands are reaching out across borders. We are learning to live together and work together as brothers and sisters on one planet.

Of course, there will always be exceptions. We can expect power-hungry individuals who will threaten peace and security in pockets of the world, but on the whole, I am greatly encouraged by the new era of freedom that is sweeping throughout the Earth.

You have freedoms—you have the freedom to change your career. You don't have to live where you're living. If it's too crowded for you, if you would like a more rural setting, then take a look at all of the glorious places God has created. Surely He will help you find your spot. If you would like a more challenging career and like the fast-paced life of a big city, then that, too, is an option open for you. Pick up the phone, get in the car, make inquiries. You never know what could be waiting for you around the corner.

You have the freedom to get an education. With all of the public education available, and with all of the financial aid programs in place in academic institutions, there is no excuse for anybody not to take a positive step toward furthering their education. Nothing is lost when a class is taken. There is everything to be gained.

You have the freedom to find fulfillment in volunteer work. There are myriads of organizations in dire need of volunteers. We rely heavily on volunteers at the Hour of Power and at the Crystal Cathedral. Every Christmas and every Easter we rely on hundreds of church members to donate their time and talent to producing the Glory of Christmas. There are hospitals and churches and civic organizations hurting for someone like you!

I have always admired Dr. Joyce Brothers. Her advice is always uplifting and positive and is supported by research. She is quick to quote a study that has been done. When I last spoke to her, she was concerned about this very subject, *Volunteerism.* What she had to say about it fascinated me.

This noted psychologist said, "Dr. Schuller, did you know that Dr. James House of the University of Michigan has research indicating that if you volunteer and work to help others, you actually live longer? We are used to our doctor saying, 'Take two aspirins and see me in the morning.' But in the future, he or she may say, 'Do some work with other people, volunteer, and see me in a week.'

"A ten year study indicates that those people who do not volunteer, who do not help others, are 2.5 times more likely to die within a period of time than those people who have physically helped others."

I was glad to hear of the research about volunteering because it scientifically supports what we preachers have been trying to teach for years. I had another question for Dr. Brothers. "Joyce, I have talked and written a great deal on the importance of goals. What do psychologists say about goals and pursuing dreams?"

"In psychology," she replied, "we have a term called goal gradient, which talks of the pulling power of the goal. Even animals show it. For example, if you put a hungry animal in a maze where there's food at the end, it will increase its running speed as it gets closer to the goal."

"In other words, a goal has an emotional magnetic power."

"Exactly. In religion, you have another term for it, don't you?"

"Well," I ventured, "We call it divine destiny."

"Yes. In psychology we tell people that if they set their specific goal, the goal will pull them toward it and, therefore, it is more likely that they will reach it."

I had to ask her one more question. "Joyce, what do you tell people whose lives are empty and vacuous? If they're living on the edge of despair or depression, what one thing could they do? What one word could you give them?"

With her usual humility she answered, "It's not my word. It's William James'. He said, 'The most important thing in life is living your life for something more important than your life.' And I think that this is where psychology and religion cross roads and come to the same point.''

Think about this and pump up your possibility thinking. You still have an exciting future going for you. Find a great cause to lose yourself in and ask God to give you a new dream and then let the dream re-shape your life. Today is a new day. You are worthy of a new dream. You are God's dream, and God don't make no junk!

#5. Realign Your Attitudes:

Tires! They sure can cost a lot. And a good friend continues to remind me that I will get many more miles from them if I keep them aligned.

I know he's right, but frequently I don't have the time to take the car down to the shop and leave it for a day while the experts fool with the tires. Not only that, but I can't tell by looking at them that they're out of alignment. And needless to say, there's always the matter of ready cash. Put all those excuses together and it's really easy to put it off 'til next week and next week and next week until it's too late. The tires are shot.

Attitudes are just as tricky. They can feel O.K. Life is going pretty smoothly. It's not necessary to read the Bible or pray. Church becomes a hassle. What to wear. Getting there on time. The family squabbles getting ready for church make you wonder if it's really worth-while.

And you read those negative articles in those well-meaning magazines, or listen to those talk shows. Sure they're interesting. You need to keep informed. They have good things to say and life is a matter of balance, isn't it?

Yes, it is! And keeping positive attitudes in your life

is a tricky balance when things are going smoothly, but run into rocky ground and it's like juggling eggs while climbing an erupting volcano. It's almost impossible to stay positive when the roof is falling in. It's pretty difficult to remain optimistic when your world is collapsing.

And yet that is what you must do. That is when you most need to keep your spirits up. You will need to realign your attitudes if you want to survive your trauma successfully.

You are reeling from a blow-out. Get out the jack and replace your negative feelings with positive attitudes. Now, it's not likely that you will be able to do this on your own. You would be better off to seek out a support group from your local hospital or church. You should certainly try to rally the support of friends, neighbors and family members. Send out an S.O.S. It's amazing how many people would love to help—if they knew you wanted help or even needed it!

THE GAME OF BLAME

Blame aimed anywhere is debilitating and will ravage your spirit. We have said that blame turned inward is shame. This destructive reaction to tragedy can be remedied with a heavy dose of tender loving care— from yourself, from your friends, from your family, your pastor and your counselor. Blame turned outward —at the world, at neighbors, at parents, children, employers, the government, at God—is just as destructive.

- "My mother made me do it."
- "They had no business closing the plant."
- "The doctors didn't care. They were negligent. If they had caught it sooner . . ."
- "It's all my husband's fault. I told him. But would he listen?"

Counselors listen for catch phrases. Phrases that include words such as *fault, blame, if only* . . . Those revealing little words and phrases signal to a counselor a person's entrapment. They are caught in the game of blame and shame. They are ensnared by an attitude of fault-finding. Who's fault is it anyway? Is it really anybody's? Who's right? Who's wrong? Is anybody ALL right? Is anybody ALL wrong? In the final analysis, does it matter?

Of course, it is important to make as few mistakes as we can in life, especially in business. We need to strive for excellence, and accountants need to aim for perfection. Those sheets had better tally, or else! But the truth of the matter is that none of us will be perfect.

All of us will make mistakes. We all do things our own way—which translates *different*—not better or worse. Because all of us function differently, because all of us make mistakes, relationships at work and at home and in the community inevitably fall into this trap of fault-finding. There is one escape from the fallout of mistakes and misunderstandings. There is one escape from accidents and their results. There is one escape from victimization—FORGIVENESS!

"LOVE YOUR NEIGHBOR—AS YOURSELF . . ."

Accidents happen. People get hurt. Lawyers are called. Accusations start to fly. Relationships and pocketbooks are strained. At times like those it's important to remember that in spite of what you are seeing and hearing, people are basically good.

We came close to a tragedy in our family last year. My daughter Sheila was driving along in their mini-van, with two of her four boys when somebody suddenly emerged from a side street and hit her full force at the rear of the car. The van spun around 360 degrees and then rolled over on its side. My daughter and my grandsons were engulfed in a shower of glass, and at the mercy of tilting, turning, crinkling metal. As the car started to turn over, Sheila thought, *This is it. This is the accident you fear will happen. It's happening. Jesus, be merciful to me and my children. They're so young. Too young to die.*

When the car stopped moving and the glass stopped flying, Sheila looked to see if her children were all right. Expecting the worst, she was relieved to see that eighteen-month-old Nicky was fine. He was hanging by his straps in his car seat, whimpering, but he appeared to be uninjured. Likewise, five-year-old Scotty hung over her, dangling from his seatbelt. They were both in one piece, with no apparent cuts or bruises.

Although the car had stopped twirling, Sheila's mind was still dazed and overwhelmed that they were all unhurt. Suddenly she saw a face peering in at her through the window. The shattered windshield was at the level of the street. A young high school student had bent down and was shouting orders at her. "Turn the engine off!"

The engine! Of course! The car was still running! She turned the key in the ignition. Then this level-headed young boy said, "Can you unlock the doors?"

She pushed the lock button on her door. She heard a click on the doors. It worked! A door above her scrunched open. It was out of her line of view. She heard a seatbelt unclick and the same controlled voice said, "We've got your baby out." Then she watched as they unstrapped Scotty and lifted him from the wreckage. "Now, can you get out?"

"I think so."

"Watch your step. Don't cut yourself on that glass. Careful. Don't bump your head."

So it went. This local "angel" walked and talked my daughter and her family out of the vehicle. In the distance sirens whirred. The firetrucks and the paramedics came, expecting to see the worst and found only a lacerated arm, that a nurse who happened to be near had wrapped in a disposable diaper. Sheila's arm had scrunched through the window and had jammed itself into the pavement. The doctors were amazed that it hadn't been severed, or broken. It required only twelve stitches.

Sheila sat helplessly on the side of the road with her two boys. The level-headed young man had kept Nicky strapped in his car seat when he had removed him from the mini-van. So Nicky was secured while paramedics tended Sheila's arm.

Another bystander asked if there was a husband who could be called. Sheila gave her Jim's work number. So this thoughtful lady called Jim and explained that although the car was totalled, his wife and children were unhurt.

When Sheila called me that night to tell me the story, she said with tears in her voice, "I am overwhelmed by the goodness of people! The people who helped me don't know me; I don't know them. I will probably never have an opportunity to tell them thank you. But I will be forever grateful to them. I will never forget their faces or the sound of their voices. I will always remember one young man who took charge for me when I could not."

People are wonderful. There is good in everyone. It may be hard to see at times. It may be clouded over by meanness or selfishness. But, within *everyone* there is an angel waiting to be released. When you can't see the goodness, when the hurt is too great, then start with forgiveness. That will lead you to see goodness.

Look at what happened to Larry Carlton.

I'll never forget watching the evening news when the newscaster announced, "Well-known jazz guitarist, Larry Carlton, is in critical condition after being shot by an unknown assailant at his home in Hollywood, California."

I had not met Larry personally, but he had married a good friend and regular vocalist at the Crystal Cathedral, Michelle Pillar. They had only been married a few months.

In the days to come we watched and prayed for Larry. It was a miracle that he had survived. We learned that the bullet had blown away his carotid artery. This brilliant musician, who had played for Sammy Davis, Jr., Michael Jackson, Linda Ronstadt, Barbra Streisand, to name a few, was attacked for no known reason. We were honored when he agreed to be a guest on the Hour of Power. And it was then that I came to know and to love this gentle, kind, loving man.

With one vocal chord left, he spoke with a low gravelly voice. He told us in his words what happened. "One day I showed up at my office, which is adjacent to my home. I saw a little dog and two boys run under the carport. The office door was ajar. I went over to shut the door so the dog wouldn't get in. As I got to the door, one of the young boys pulled out a gun and shot me in the neck."

"How far was he from you?"

"About twelve feet."

"Was the shooting unprovoked?"

"Oh, yes," he said, "It was just one of those random shootings that you hear about. My eyes met the boy's eyes before he turned and ran. I managed to walk about fifteen feet to the service porch area where

I laid down on the linoleum. My secretary found me and she immediately called 911.

"As I was laying there bleeding, I was sure that I was dying. I prayed, 'Jesus, forgive me of my sins, and let's go home.' "

"But Jesus wasn't ready to take you home."

"No. I lost about eleven liters of blood. It took four hours of surgery to repair my carotid artery. And miraculously, the bullet virtually missed every nerve that has anything to do with my arm. It traumatized those nerves, but there was no permanent damage. My arm was paralyzed. It's still numb throughout, but it's going to be completely healed, in time. And I'm beginning to play again."

"Larry, you have said that you weren't a Christian when you were playing for all of these superstars. Yet, you have credited God with the fact that you are alive today and that you still have the use of your arm. When did God become a real force in your life?"

"It was in 1983. I had spent many years discussing philosophy and religion. I would sneak a peak at a Christian station and if somebody would walk into the room, I would change the channel. The Holy Spirit was working on me for a long time. One evening, in a hotel room in New York City after a concert, I was alone, reading some books. I spoke my first words to Jesus. I said, 'I don't know any more about you than I did two years ago, but I choose you, Jesus.' As a result of that prayer the Lord started changing my life."

"So God prepared you for the shooting by giving you a faith beforetime. That faith carried you through when you were lying alone and bleeding, and in the times of recovery."

"Yes. I have such gladness that I chose Jesus on the moment that I was dying. It reinforces in my heart how much I love the Lord, even though I fail daily, as we all do.''

"Larry, they have never found the assailant, in spite of a substantial reward. How do you feel about the boy who shot you?''

"Well, I think God had prepared me for this, because I honestly feel sorry that we have children out there like that boy. There are children who wake up one day and they decide they are going to take a gun and go out and shoot someone. So I have sympathy for our society that we're breeding this kind of child. But anger? No. He's a poor kid, you know.''

Larry's been hurt, but he's chosen to forgive the child and the society that bred such a child. He has chosen to let go of the anger and the rage. And what a wise choice it has been. If you could look Larry in the eyes, as I have, you would see a gentle, kind, caring, loving soul. He is alive today in more ways than one.

You have been hurt too. Perhaps not in such a dramatic way. But it is well-known that our world is full of victims these days. They are victims of abuse and injustice. Pain is a natural by-product. *But seething rage, unresolved anger is a poor and a dangerous child.*

How do you change these feelings? Start with forgiveness. That's the first step toward healing. You were hurt. You didn't deserve to be hurt. Don't add rage and unresolved anger to the pile of pain you already have. Start cleaning up the debris by being willing to say, "I forgive you."

Boy! That's a hard one. But it can be done. It will take some work and more directions than I want to get into here. We will explore the issue of forgiveness in more depth in the seventh chapter, for we all have people in our lives who have hurt us. We all carry some baggage of unresolved anger. It may be deep in our subconscious where we have buried it, hoping it will go away. Of course it doesn't and rears its ugly head in weak moments of injustice and frustration. We can learn to cope with these feelings.

LIFE'S NOT FAIR, BUT GOD IS GOOD!

I run into cynics, skeptics, agnostics, atheists and they say: *If there was a good God, why does this evil have to happen?*

Can we blame God for evil in the world? Did He create it? Of course not! God becomes a handy excuse for us to hang our complaints on. He did create human beings—creatures with free wills to do good—or evil. If we didn't have the freedom to make bad choices, we also couldn't make good choices. Unfortunately, sometimes people do make bad choices and the result is unfair to us, but in spite of this unfairness, God is good.

Look at the case of a California doctor. I first met Serena Young when reading the *Los Angeles Times*. I opened the paper and saw a picture of a tiny doctor propped on crutches, performing orthopaedic surgery. As I read the story, a couple of tears rolled down my cheeks. I wrote this remarkable young woman and was surprised to get a beautiful letter back from her. In it she related how my books had helped her. I called her and said, "Serena, we have to meet."

So she graciously agreed to come to the Crystal Cathedral and shared her story with others in the hopes that it would give hope to them. Serena is today the Assistant Orthopedic Surgeon chief on the Adult Brain Injury Service at Rancho Los Amigos. This is a long way from where she was born.

Serena was born in Taipei, Taiwan, of Chinese heritage. Then, at the age of two, in 1957, Serena contracted polio. Whereas the vaccine was readily available in the United States at that time, it was not so in Taiwan. When Serena woke up one morning, she was not able to move a muscle below her neck. She remembers her mother telling her to get out of bed but she just couldn't move.

At first her mother thought she was playing around, but when she put her hand on Serena's forehead, she could feel the high fever.

I asked Serena, "You were two at the time? Do you remember any of this?"

"Oh, yes! In fact, the next thing I remember, I was in a hospital, and my mother was kneeling by my bed. She was praying. She later told me that she had asked God that if He would bring me back, that she would dedicate my life to Him."

"And you did get better."

"Yes."

"And how did you get from there to America?"

Pretty Serena remembered it all. She said, "Well, after I survived the crisis, my parents brought me to a lot of medical specialists in Taiwan. I had all kinds of treatments, ranging from ancient Chinese herbs to acupuncture. And over the ensuing year, I regained strength in my upper extremity, but my legs remained paralyzed. My father had heard that the medical technology was far more advanced in the United States. He was working for the American Embassy at that time in Taiwan, so he petitioned the government to let our family immigrate. After two years, in 1959, our family was granted permission to immigrate to the United States."

"Now, when did you get the dream of becoming a surgeon?"

"When I got to the United States, I became a patient at Orthopaedic Hospital in Los Angeles. Within a year's time, they put me in braces and crutches and I

There Are

VAST
UNTAPPED
RESOURCES

Of Faith . . .
And Talent . . .

THAT CAN
ONLY BE
DISCOVERED
IN ADVERSITY!

was walking! So I was really impressed with orthopae-dics at a very young age. I was in and out of the hospi-tal between the ages of four to twenty-one. But the thought of becoming an orthopaedic surgeon really did not occur to me until high school."

Serena seemed so sweet and happy. It was hard to believe that this woman had ever gone through the trials that she had endured. I asked her, "Were you ever bitter about this whole experience?"

Her answer surprised me, but I loved her honesty. I felt that she spoke for millions of people. "I was very bitter and angry at God, because I thought that if God was truly a loving God, how could He allow this tragedy to happen to me? How could He allow sickness and disease in this world? And for a long time, I was really angry and I couldn't figure out the answers.

"One summer during high school, I volunteered at Orthopaedic Hospital. I worked with handicapped children. At first their deformed bodies really both-ered me. I went home and I couldn't figure out why it bothered me so. I finally realized that the reason why it bothered me was because I couldn't accept my own physical deformity. That caused me to start searching.

"I started wondering if there was even really a God and how could any of this make sense? In my search, I started to read the Bible, and there was one verse that really stuck out in my mind. It was in Romans 8:28, which says, 'And we know that all things work together for good to those who love God, to those who are the called according to His purpose.'

"That meant that ALL things work together for the good. Did that mean that my tragedy actually could work for my good? Well, I started praying about it, and I challenged God. I said, 'God, if You're real, I want You to use this tragedy to make it something good.'

"That's when He helped me get over my disability.

He helped me accept it. And that's when I started to have a desire to help other people with disabilities. It was during that summer that I decided I wanted to be an orthopaedic surgeon."

I said to this remarkable young woman, "And did you get encouragement on your decision to become an orthopaedic surgeon?"

"Oh, no! I was told that I had to be out of my mind even to consider the thought! But I just had a real conviction in my heart. I really felt that this was my calling, that God was giving me—giving me the desire. There were times during my residency where I really wanted to quit. There was a point where I really thought I was not gonna make it. But, God gave me a husband that never stopped believing in me."

I looked into bright, sparkling dark eyes. Glistening black hair. A radiant smile. I said, "The picture of you in the paper showed you propped up on crutches leaning over an operating table. Is the job worth all the effort it took you to get there? You hung in there. You never quit. You got through with all of the challenges that you faced. Now you're there. Is it worth the price you paid?"

"My career is more fulfilling than I thought it could ever be. The price was really high, but it's really been worth it. There are rewards. I spend part of my time on the Adult Brain Injury Service at Rancho Los Amigos Medical Center. Most of these patients are between the ages of eighteen and twenty-five. It's really unfortunate, because a lot of their injuries could have been prevented. These patients sustained head injuries from car accidents or motorcycle accidents. And, you know, if they would have just put on their seat belts, or maybe wore helmets when they were riding their motorcycles, maybe they could have prevented their head injuries. I also spend one day a week at Long Beach

Veterans Administration Hospital where I'm part of a special team for Amputations Mobility and Prosthetics. And this is where I become involved with helping veterans with amputations or foot and ankle problems."

I was amazed. Here stood a living testimony to the power of God's grace. A mother prayed for a dying little girl. A loving God delivered her from bitterness and replaced it with a magic, marvelous, miraculous dream, and now she is healing, helping, operating, repairing.

LIFE'S NOT FAIR, BUT DON'T BLAME GOD!

It was headline news: *Pitcher Makes Miraculous Comeback.* All eyes were focused on Candlestick Park where Dave Dravecky was pitching for the San Francisco Giants. He had pitched several shut-out games. His career had just begun to take off when he was handed the grim news that he carried a malignant tumor in his deltoid muscle. Of all places where the tumor could have been—it had to be in his arm, and not just any arm—his pitching arm.

The type of cancer found in Dave's muscle was not considered life-threatening, but it would definitely kill his career, said the doctors. Because the cancer has such a high incidence of recurrence, the doctors stripped him of half of his powerful deltoid muscle. Then, for an added measure of insurance, they froze the bone to inhibit growth of any more cancer cells on the membrane lining of the bone.

According to pure physics, it would be impossible for him ever to throw a baseball again, much less pitch. A career in the majors was out of the question—to everyone but Dave. He was determined to make a comeback. Quietly, without fanfare, he worked out. He began to throw the baseball. "How did you do that?"

his doctors asked him. "You can't do that without a deltoid."

Encouraged by the positive reaction he received from his doctors and his trainers, Dave continued to develop the remaining muscles in his arm and especially in his shoulder. He dreamed, visualized, worked toward a comeback. He did the impossible. He threw a baseball. He increased his speed and his control. Now he only had to convince the management.

Impressed by what they saw, the Giants decided to give Dave a try. They sent him down to the minors to see how his arm would perform under the pressure of real competition. Dave shone. His pitches zinged over the plate and befuddled many a batter. Champing at the bit, Dave longed to help out his team as they struggled to win the league championship. Finally all of his work and effort paid off. He got the call to fly to San Francisco. He would start the game the next night.

The newspapers got a hold of the story. The stadium was bombarded with reporters, cameras, microphones. The whole world was poised and watching. Everyone was rooting for Dave. Everyone wanted this miracle to come true. They wanted to see him win over the odds. They wanted to see him pitch—and WIN!

On August 10, 1989, Dave stepped out onto the field to thunderous applause. The screen lit up the field with ten-foot high letters, "WELCOME BACK, DAVE!"

Here, in his own words, is how Dave described the moment:

"God had given me the opportunity to come back against all odds and play a game that I love so much. I had been listening to a special song on the way to the stadium, *Give thanks with a grateful heart. Give thanks to the Holy One. Give thanks because He's given Jesus Christ His only Son.* As I stood there on the mound, I took the first thirty seconds to think about the words of that song and what they meant to me. I was overwhelmed with the thanks that I have for God for allowing me to come back, but more important was the miracle of salvation that occurred in my life some eight years earlier when I met Jesus Christ as my Lord and Savior.

"Other than that I remember three things. The first pitch was a ball, because I wanted to keep that ball. The second was I struck out Ron Oester and for the first time in my career I showed emotion. The third was when Luis Quinones hit a home run and Terry Kennedy yelled at him and said, 'You dummy, you just messed up the script.' "

Everybody wanted Dave to win, but the Cincinnati Reds weren't about to give him the victory. They were fighting a battle for the pennant. They fought the Giants, but Dave proved to be a tough pitcher—with or without a deltoid. It was the sweetest victory of his life and offered hope to the millions who watched him.

The newspapers wildly proclaimed the miracle. No one doubted that Dave had done the impossible. He gave credit to God. The newspapers reported Dave's incredible faith. But five days later as Dave pitched against Montreal, his fragile, frozen, brittle bone broke, flinging Dave to the ground in agony.

It was his last time pitching for the majors. There would not be a second comeback. There would be no more pitching. The world was stunned. How could a miracle be so short-lived? How would Dave Dravecky react to his God, the One who supposedly gave him the miracle in the first place? Would he be bitter? Was the miracle all a mistake? How could anyone believe in a God who could be so cruel?

Those questions and many, many more were bantered around press rooms, bars, locker rooms, living rooms. The world watched and waited to see how this bright young man would react. All those months of hard work—for what? One game? Was it worth it?

I sent Dave a telegram, as did thousands and thousands of people. I prayed for him. God had something powerful He wanted to say through Dave Dravecky. As I watched and listened to the media, I could see how wisely God had chosen His spokesperson. Rarely, in my years of pastoring people and providing hope to the hopeless, have I seen such unwavering faith as I saw in Dave those weeks following his devastating injury.

Months later, I had the chance to talk to him and ask him some of the questions that I had longed to ask him. When we did meet, the first question I asked was, "Did you ever experience low times, Dave? It would have been perfectly natural considering the difficult blows you had to endure."

He gazed at me with sure, steady dark eyes. His face was serene. Without the slightest hesitation he said, "Well, as I look back over this entire experience, I would honestly say that I had very few low days. I have been at peace through this whole thing knowing that God is in complete control of my life. I'm not going to say that it's been a bed of roses and that everything has gone well.

"There were times when I was preparing for my comeback when I was very frustrated, but the most important thing for me at that point was to be as prepared as I could be and then allow God to take care of the rest. If I were to fail and not make it, I knew that God had a better plan for Dave Dravecky. During my training, I struggled at times and my wife, Janice, had all she could do to get me to go to therapy. I knew it was all worth it because I learned to trust in God completely."

"Dave, you have been an inspiration to millions of people here in America as well as in other countries.

How did you keep such an unwavering faith? I mean, it would have been so easy for you to have been bitter at God. Most of us would have said, *Why, God? Why did my tumor have to have been in my pitching arm? Why couldn't it have been in my other arm? Or why did you let me see a comeback, just to come crashing down on the mound five days later? Why did you let me work so hard, so many months, just for one game?* How did you handle such natural questions?"

He replied, "When you look at life, there are so many trials and setbacks that people face. When I was at Sloan Kettering, I saw so many people who were in worse shape than I was. But one of the most comforting things for me was realizing that it wasn't the end result that I was looking for. It was the process which I was going through and that process was walking with God every day. It was seeing how He was working things out in my life and ultimately drawing me closer to Him."

Dave added, "You know, life isn't fair. People can't expect always to see things peaches and cream and rosy. There are going to be times when we have a setback, but through trust in Jesus Christ we can have the peace to be content in the midst of the storm and that's what I experienced during that period of time— that peace in the midst of the storm."

Dave's faith really taught me a lot. I responded to his comments, "So your trust in Jesus Christ didn't change the situation as much as it changed your attitude toward it. Would that be correct?"

"Most definitely. I had two choices. One choice was to give in to the despair to the point where I would not be able to endure this. My other choice was to put my faith and trust in Jesus Christ who was in control of my life. I decided to choose the latter path and enjoy what I was going through even though it may have been difficult. In retrospect, it has been a wonderful journey. It's been a blessing from God.''

He added, "I just believe that God had a purpose and a plan for my life. His hand was on me. I don't know all the mysteries of God, but for some reason, God wanted me to pitch. That was God's plan for me and through my cancer I see that there is something greater He is calling me to. It is bigger than baseball. It is a relationship with God that He is directing. I am really grateful that I got a chance to play major league baseball. Many boys dream of it. I actually got the chance. That means a lot to me.''

How exciting to meet someone who is LIVING what the Bible has taught for centuries. I asked him to elaborate for those who are new to the concepts. I said, "Some people don't understand. They can't relate to what you said. They say, 'A lot of good Jesus did for you. You had all that talent and here you are—all washed up as a pitcher.' ''

"What those people don't realize is that it's not what I've given up, but what I've gained. I can rest in the fact that I have faith not in what is seen here in the temporary, but in what is unseen, that which is eternal and that's where my faith rests. It's in that eternal promise that God gives us through a relationship with Jesus Christ.''

"When you say, you trust in Jesus Christ, do you actually talk to Him?''

"Most definitely. I pray to Him and He responds through the people He has placed around me. One of the important things I learned about the Bible was in seeking wise counsel from friends and fellow believers. I've experienced peace through the prayers of others and I've seen God actually answer my prayers through those people.''

"That must mean a great deal to you, especially

when you're so young and when this cancer continues to return. Correct?''

"Yes. It recently flared up again." (Dave has since had to have his arm amputated.)

I looked at this handsome, smiling athlete, husband, father. "What does your future hold for you, Dave? What are your dreams? Your goals? Your hopes?''

"My dreams and my hopes are to serve God wherever I go and in whatever I do. I don't know what He has planned for me, but I love God with all my heart and all I want to do is serve Him."

Dave's story is detailed in an exciting book entitled *Comeback* (Zondervan). In the book Dave made this statement: "Life's not fair, but let's not confuse life with God."

I read that statement. I met with Dave. That week I made a pastoral visit to a dying friend. My wife and I prayed with this shriveled woman, racked with the pain of cancer. It was the day before Easter. I said to her, "Life's not fair, but God is good."

"Oh, Bob," she exclaimed, "That's so true!"

That simple statement has developed into a book—this book—and in retrospect I began to realize that the seeds for this book were planted by a dynamic young pitcher. "Life's not fair, but let's not confuse life with God." In other words, "Life's not fair, but God is good!"

Yes He is. God is good. He doesn't create the problems—He redeems them. He doesn't make the mistakes—He fixes them. He doesn't cause cancer. He heals. He doesn't kill dreams or bodies. He gives life. He gives the big picture—the ability to see beyond this temporal setback to a glorious comeback!

You can be a living, loving testimony that life's not fair—but God is good!

CHAPTER THREE

• —————————————————————————— •

Disappointed? Yes.
Discouraged? Sometimes.
Defeated? Never!

All Gone, but Not Done In!

The whole nation grieved for Crest Hills, Joliet, and Plain-field, Illinois, the tiny towns devastated by a tornado in late August of 1990. The pictures on the broadcasts brought the grim news to those of us in California, Hawaii, Alaska, New York City. A newscaster interviewed a man who had lost his home in the tornado. This homeless man stood in the midst of the rubble and said to the reporter, "It's all gone! It's all gone! There's nothing left!"

Those words struck a vibrant chord in my memory bank. I recalled the day as if it were yesterday. I had returned home from college for summer vacation. It was a hot, humid summer day, typical weather for Iowa that time of year. The air was so close and thick that I felt as though I was going to suffocate.

I longed for relief from the heat, or at least a fresh breeze to stir up the air. The sky grew black. A warm wind blew in through the fields. It rustled its way through the rows of corn, rattled the barn doors, and blew dust through the open windows of the old farmhouse. The barn doors trembled on their hinges. The curtains flapped hauntingly. There was no doubt about it. A storm was brewing.

Dad said simply, "It looks like hail."

Nothing was more threatening to roses. Delicate leaves and petals are no match against an onslaught of icy pellets. We got out the old buckets to cover the rose plants. Suddenly the air grew deathly still.

The sudden change startled us. We lifted our heads to the sky and saw it—an ominous dark cloud stretched into the shape of a long, slithering black snake. It dropped its poisonous head to the earth and struck in a cloud of dust! It moved across the land with alarming speed. We had no way to defend ourselves against a tornado. Our only chance was to run away, hopefully fast enough.

We leaped into the car and fled in a cloud of dust down the old gravel road. Then, as quickly as it appeared, the black, serpentine cloud periscoped its way back into the sky and disappeared.

We were safe! We could go back home. The old Chevy rumbled up the dirt road and approached the hill that hid our farm home. We always knew we were close to home when we reached this hill because you could see the tip of the old red barn peeking over the top of the hill. But that day there was no sign of a barn rising above the hill. Dad kept his foot to the pedal, hoping his eyes would see what his heart feared was gone. At the crest of the hill we saw the devastating damage. The monster cloud had devoured the entire farm. Every building was gone.

The tornado had swept up the house, the barn and all the other buildings. Like some monstrous vacuum cleaner, it had sucked them away and dropped them in an unwelcomed heap on the neighbor's farm.

All of Dad's years of hard work had been leveled, destroyed in one fell swoop. He gripped the steering wheel with his well-worn hands. The gnarled knuckles turned white with rage. This silent, gentle man began to beat the steering wheel. Bitter tears crept across his stubbly cheeks. "It's all gone, Jenny!" he cried. "It's all gone!"

IT WAS ALL GONE! What a devastating blow! I looked at my father. What a bitter disappointment! Disappointed? Yes! Discouraged? Definitely not. Disappointments are life's realities. Discouragement is a human reaction.

Dad was not about to take this setback lying down. He refused to be discouraged. Instead, he chose to be challenged. He still had fight left in him. Sure, it was all gone. ALL GONE! But we were not done in! We still had recovery power within us.

We managed to find shelter that night with relatives. Then we heard about a house in town that was being demolished. It was being cleared to make way for a new one. The owners said we could have the materials if we would take the house apart and clear the lot for the new building. What a deal! No ball and chain for us! We carefully pried one board from another. We peeled off the wood siding, one plank at a time. The studs and beams were carefully saved, and then we extracted and straightened every nail. Those salvaged supplies built a new house on the same farm where the original house had stood.

ALL GONE! BUT NOT DONE IN! The new house served Mom and Dad well until my older brother Henry got married. Then, as is the custom in those parts, my parents moved to town to allow Henry and his wife a chance to take over the farm. The newlyweds lived in that house for forty years!

All Gone? Perhaps! But Not Done In!
Disappointed? Absolutely!
But Not Defeated!

Thinking back on my parents' experience in the tornado, I can say of them, "Disappointed? Yes. Defeated? Never! In the face of what looked like defeat, he turned his experience into a challenge. He allowed God to show His love and mercy.

Life's not fair but God is good.

Life throws us a disappointment—and God responds by giving us encouragement.

Everyone faces disappointments at one time or another—but the winners are the ones who refuse to let the disappointments become discouragements. Success isn't a matter of being the best. Success is a matter of handling the worst. It is being able to deal constructively with life's disappointments.

Who are the winners? Who are these people who refuse to be done in, who refuse to be defeated by their disappointments? How do they take their losses and turn them into gains?

Four ways: 1) *They think positively.* 2) *They live positively.* 3) *They work positively.* 4) *They pray positively.* It's really so simple.

THINK POSITIVELY

I have always been amazed at how powerful the thinking process is. Did you know that your life can be greatly affected just by the way you think? You can think negatively or positively. If you are a positive thinker, you will base your decisions on faith rather than fear. When you think positively, you will be a happy person, a delightful person to live with, work with and be around. The positive thinkers are happier and even healthier. Scientists have shown that positive thinking releases endorphins, which promote a healthier body.

Positive thinking has so many benefits and positive side effects. Conversely, negative thinking steals joy, blinds happiness, robs health, promotes decay and even death.

THINK about it! There's no good reason why thoughts should be negative instead of positive. And yet, there's no question about it, the majority of the people living today suffer from negative thinking. It's a deadly disease. It destroys families, sabotages well-laid plans in education, athletics, business and academic pursuits. It destroys millions and millions of dreams each year.

Negative thinking is subtle and deceptive. It wears many faces, and hides behind a variety of masks. It may appear as *realism*. It may construct an elaborate facade of *practicality*. This clever chameleon loves to don the costume of *laziness*. It loves to hide behind the mask of *excuses*.

If positive thinking has so many benefits, whereas negative thinking carries so much harmful baggage, WHY do people continue to think, "I can't!"

Strip away the masks, burn the costumes, tear down the facades, discover the real, root emotion. Behind the excuses, laziness, practicality, realism, and other guises of negative thinking is—FEAR.

People are negative because they are afraid. They are afraid of being disappointed. Call it the fear of dashed hopes. Call it the fear of having your dreams turn to ashes. Call it the fear of failure.

"I don't want to be disappointed. So I don't think I'll try." That's negative thinking. That's fearful thinking.

Now if you could learn how to deal with disappointments, if you could learn to lose without being defeated, would you dare to think positively?

If you will learn how to be disappointed without being discouraged, you need never be defeated. You'll never experience final failure. You will set higher goals. You will try again. When you realize that the worst that can happen is that you may have to face a disappointment, then you will be transformed from a doubter to a believer, from a negative thinker to a positive thinker.

Learn from the experts. Every four years you'll find the greatest collection of expert positive thinkers congregating. They hold their international conference in a different city of a different country. This global gathering of positive thinkers is the most watched televised event in the world. Hundreds of millions of people arrange their schedules to watch and listen to these positive thinkers. You say you've never heard of it? Sure you have.

The Olympics are one of the greatest conglomerates of positive thinkers you will ever hope to find. Every four years, the world is treated with one story after another of positive thinkers who have dared to believe that they can beat the odds and come home with the ultimate prize—the GOLD MEDAL!

I cannot get enough of the Olympics. I wish they could be held every year, for they continually inspire me and encourage me to try harder. Take Janet Evans, for example. Janet is the gold medal swimmer from Placentia, California, and a member of the Crystal Cathedral. She stood in the pulpit there only days after her victorious return from Seoul, Korea, where she won three gold medals.

Janet holds three world records, one in the 400 meter freestyle, one for the 800 meter freestyle, and the 1,500 meter! I asked her if I could see one of her medals. She humbly showed it to me and said, "You can hold it if you like."

"Would I like!" I was thrilled to feel the weight of the gleaming medal dangle from my fingertips. It was much heavier than I thought it would be. What a prize! What a symbol of a woman's ability to think positively, dream big, and work hard.

I reluctantly returned the medal to this bright, cheery young girl. She looked so young to have come so far. I said to her, "You are a success. There's no doubt about it. No one can argue with that fact. You are an expert positive thinker. Your accomplishments are proof of that. Many people would like to know how did you get to be so successful?"

Well, I must confess. I had predicted that Janet would say, "It was all of those positive messages I heard while I was growing up in the Crystal Cathedral." But she had an even better response. This tiny, petite, bright-eyed young girl said, "I could not have done it without my family. They supported me. My mother, my father, and my brothers—they were there behind me, helping me all the way."

According to this positive thinking expert, family is key to success. That insight intrigued me. I wanted to find out more about her family and how it contributed to her success. "How did your family influence you in your swimming career?"

Her reply was practical enough. "I swam because my brothers did. I learned when I was a baby. They started swimming on a swim team, so I followed them and started swimming competitively when I was four."

"Did you make that decision, or did your father and mother make it for you?"

Without batting an eye, Janet replied, "It was my decision. My brothers were doing it, and I wanted to do whatever they were doing."

"When did you get the idea to work toward the Olympics?" I asked.

"Oh, I always had little goals along the way, and then when I was twelve years old, I won my first Junior National Championship. Then, in 1986, I decided that if I worked really hard and did the best I could, then I could probably go to the Olympics."

I was beginning to get the picture. Family provided a safe place. A safe place gave Janet the courage to risk failure. It gave her the freedom to dream dreams and set goals. I was learning a lot from this positive thinking expert. I probed further. "Is it true that everything nice has its price?"

"Oh, yes!"

"Have you ever, along the way, had any disappointments that you had to overcome so you could keep going?"

This unassuming, modest, unaffected young girl replied, "Of course. Often my swimming pre-empted other things I wanted to do. It took many hours of my life. Also, there were swimming meets when I was disappointed in my performance. I didn't swim as well as I thought I could. Afterward I told myself to work harder and do better next time. The next time always motivated me to keep on trying."

Wow! Here was a brilliant new insight into positive thinking: THE "NEXT TIME" ALWAYS MOTIVATED ME TO KEEP ON TRYING!

No wonder Janet is a winner's winner! And watch

out! She plans to keep winning! This positive thinking expert has more next times planned.

Don't get the wrong impression. Positive thinkers don't always win. They don't always bring home the medals. Sometimes they don't even make it to the final round. That's one of the realities of positive thinking. That's why it's no Pollyanna philosophy. Positive thinking experts know that years of work, even a lifetime of sacrifice and dedication can reap historical rewards, but there are no guarantees.

The fine line that separates the winners from the losers can be as minimal as a hundredth of a second! Then there are debilitating injuries that can shelf a career for good. For those athletes there will be no more next times. Those contenders have devoted their young lives to pursuing this elusive dream, only to miss out on the final prize. The acute disappointment can only be imagined.

Yet, I have known many positive thinking people who have not let even such debilitating disappointments defeat them. For instance, there are the Hayden twins, Dan and Dennis.

We were all invited to the lovely birthday party of Kenny Rogers in Hollywood, California. We sat next to each other at the same table only two days after a "sudden death" injury that eliminated these twins from what was an eight-year campaign to go to the Olympics. They were the gymnastics hopefuls for the 1988 Olympics. International champions, the world was watching them with glee and trepidation (depending on which country they lived in). Then, while competing in the qualifying trials for the Olympics team, Dan tore a muscle. Even as his shoulder touched mine at dinner he was in such pain he could not stand to spread the butter on his dinner roll. Three days before he was the favorite to win the gold in Seoul! He now knew that he would not even be going to Korea! And in fact he would never compete—ever again! Since the age of six his sights were set on the Olympics. Now—everything was history! Yet, his disappointments were not turned into discouragements.

I asked these two identical brothers, "How did you get into gymnastics?"

"We have four older brothers," Dan replied. "Dennis and I used to have strength contests with our brothers. We started winning those strength contests when we were six years old, so our parents told our brothers to take us to the YMCA where we could put some of that energy to constructive use."

Was I hearing a recurring theme? Family. First Janet mentioned it, now the Haydens. It seemed that a positive family was the launching pad for venturing into new arenas. I could see where it is extremely important to have people around you who care about you whether or not you won or lost. The twins had each other as well as a large family and they could support each other and encourage each other while competing in a very narrow range of success.

Life deals in a wide variety of measures. Some achievements are weighed on a broad scale, others on a narrow scale. It seems to me that the wider range offers more possibilities for success. The narrow range offers more possibilities for failure. Hence it requires great courage and a firm support system to dare to compete in the narrow range. When it comes to International Gymnastics competitions, I had always heard the range was extremely narrow. I asked the twins, "Is it true that the margin between winning and losing in gymnastics is slim?"

The brothers laughed and said, "Oh, definitely. In fact, in 1985, Dennis and I competed for the top collegiate team at Arizona State, Dr. Schuller, under your friend, Don Robinson. We missed the team finals by .05. Then in 1986 we *won* by .05. That's called the winner's edge—which is often very thin."

"It must take great courage to compete in an arena where the margin of success is so slim."

"It does. But it is much more exciting to win in that arena, than it is to lose in one where success is easier to attain."

These twins beamed with positive thinking. It was obvious that they were close and supportive. No sibling rivalry here. That close-knit relationship really held them up when their soaring careers came to a crashing halt in Salt Lake City. The world was watching when it happened. I asked them about it.

Dan cleared his throat. It was not easy to talk about. "My shoulder had been bothering me before final trials. It was aggravating me in my workouts. I wasn't able to train the way I needed to or wanted to for the final trials. Going into the final trials, my shoulder progressively got worse.

"I had just won the USA championships, ranking me as the number one male gymnast in the country. I won three gold medals on the events. On the second to last event in the finals, my shoulder separated. I felt it tear. I stopped right in the middle of my routine. I went to my coach. I said, 'Ed, I think my shoulder separated.' He told me, 'You have two more events. You need to complete this event. Just give it your best shot.'

"I went through the parallel bar routine with pain. I scored 93. Usually I score a 98 or 99 because it's one of my better events. I made it through. I was happy.

"In the last event, I do a move called the Kovaks which is extremely difficult to do even when you are a hundred percent. I did the first Kovaks in my routine. I still had a lot of pain. I missed the first Kovaks. I let go of the front of the bar and did a one and a half back flip over the bar. I was supposed to recatch the bar. I missed the catch. I chalked up and looked behind me at my old coach, Kenichi. He said, 'Go again, go again.' I looked at my new coach, Ed, and he agreed, 'Yes, go one more time.'

"So I got up. I tried the Kovaks again and again. I didn't succeed. I finished my routine and then I sat down. I knew I had big problems with my shoulder. I knew I had not scored high enough to win.

"I began to talk to myself. My conversation with myself went like this: *Why, Lord?* No, don't ask why. Ask how. *O.K., how am I going to get through this?*

"I kept faith in the Lord, and that really helped. If I didn't have the Lord at that time, I would have really been crushed, but He gave me strength and courage."

Dennis also suffered an injury that kept him from competing. Dan and Dennis Hayden, the two top contenders for gold medals, never made it to the final competition. They both got knocked out by debilitating injuries. They were never able to compete again. Years and years of work—for nothing. Life's not fair!

Disappointed? You bet!

Defeated? Never! For God is good. His spirit moves through the positive thinking mind and instead of discouragement there's a spirit of hope—or peace! Or new challenges! They never gave into that destructive WHY? Instead they grasped onto the renewing HOW? HOW would they accept this injury? HOW would they face up to the disappointment? HOW would they dare to dream again?

The answer was found in the fact that they "belonged." They had each other, they had a family, and they had a positive faith. These positive thinkers dared to look disappointment in the eyes. They put themselves in risky situations; they risked disappointment,

DISAPPOINTED?
You Bet!

DISCOURAGED?
A Little.

DEFEATED?
Never!

because they knew that if life slammed the door in their face, God would give them a new goal!

Their fear of failure was diffused by a very important ingredient. They have a strong, supportive family behind them, EN-Courage-ing them. They have faith in God, in their Lord.

Do you want to have the courage to become a positive thinker? You'll find it when you become connected to someone who will support you. It helps if it's family. But it doesn't have to be a blood connection. It can be any one who is willing to be an en-courager, someone who will give you the courage to risk failure. Look anywhere—you'll find a support system. Look at the church. Look at the local hospital. Call the local university. Check your neighborhood. The support systems are there. Nobody has to go it alone. Indeed, it is doubtful that anybody could make it alone.

PLAN POSITIVELY

When life hands you a big disappointment, when your dreams blow up in your face, it's time to make new plans. It's not time to run away, give up, or cash in, but it is time to get a positive plan on how you are going to handle this disappointment.

A plan is all-important, and it cannot be just any plan; it needs to be a POSITIVE plan! I've said it once; I'll say it again, WHEN YOU FAIL TO PLAN YOU PLAN TO FAIL.

Handsome, athletic, intelligent—David Cornelson was on top of the world. He had earned his B.A. from Boston University and his Master's Degree in Religion from Yale University, and was working on his Doctorate from the University of Pennsylvania. He had been captain of the Yale cycling team and raced with the United States Cycling Federation. Then, the accident happened. His car crashed head-on into an oncoming vehicle. He was left paralyzed.

Like most victims of tragic accidents that have permanent results, David went through the first phase of recovery—denial. He denied that the injuries were permanent. He believed that this condition was temporary. When it was clear that the injury was irreversible, he had to accept the extent of the injury. He held on for a long time to the hope that he would get back more function as time passed. He clung to the faint possibility that he would heal to some extent.

Once he knew that his life had been forever, permanently altered, that he would never walk again, much less run, or cycle, he entered the mourning phase. He told me, "That is probably the hardest point, because you're reminiscing about the past. You're feeling nostalgic about the way you used to be. There was a lot of glorification about what it was like to walk and to run."

I looked at the good-looking young man, who has studied the human spirit in depth within the disciplines of the educational system. More than that, he has lived through one of the most devastating blows the human spirit can endure. I said to him, "David, I think you are right when you say that this is the hardest phase. I have seen many people get stuck there. They get mired in the mourning. They don't have the wherewithal to get through it. What did you do to get through the mourning?"

"Well," he replied, "The mourning phase is a very lonely process. It pretty much has to be done by yourself. The private side of me felt comfort by writing in a journal. When I was feeling in utter despair, when I felt overwhelmed by the grief, I would pray and I would write. In the process a glimmer of light would shine. For example, here are some excerpts from my journal:

"This was written on March 5, 1988, shortly after I was released from the hospital and had confronted this strange new world:

> The psychological pain is enormous, almost unbearable at times. I think of suicide often. I don't know what to do with myself. I feel desperate. I wish I could just sleep and be the whole person in my dreams. Knowing what it is like to be whole for all those years and now to be disabled is so difficult to accept.
>
> Why did this have to happen? Why can't my body recover from it? Why can't medical science do something to heal me before I destroy myself?

"A candid excerpt," I commented. "You sound like there were times when the will to die was stronger than the will to live."

"Oh, yes!" he said. "I never made specific plans, but I was unable to see enough meaning and purpose to want to go on the way I was."

"What was the turning point?"

"It was more than a single moment. It was a gradual process. I think this excerpt illustrates a healing point. I wrote this prayer in my journal at a very vulnerable point:

> Dear Lord, as I near another night of sleep, please grant me a sound sleep and peaceful dreams. Please, Father, I pray that You find me worthy of the Spirit and forgive me of my weakness and my sins. Heal my soul, and give me the strength to endure throughout this life. Lead me onward, giving direction and purpose to my life. I pray for ongoing love and closeness with my family. And I pray and hope that families can, indeed, be re-

united after death. Carry me gently through trying times. I need You most then. I love You, Lord, and yearn to know You, yet feel so far away and alone at times. Please help. I say these things in the name of Jesus Christ. Amen.

"And did God answer that prayer?" I asked.

"Definitely. I began to move out of the mourning phase, into the adjusting phase. I began to move beyond and to look beyond. I began to set new goals."

"Such as?"

"It all started when I got my first racing wheelchair. They are constructed lighter than a normal chair. Because of that chair I began to enter wheelchair races. Through those races I met John Moreno who was with the Ultra Marathon Cycling Association. He began to challenge me. He asked me, 'David, have you ever thought of going cross country on a hand cycle?'

"I shook my head. I was not interested in being considered as a disabled athlete. Undaunted, he proceeded to tell me about Bob Whelan who cycled across the United States from coast to coast on a hand cycle in thirty-five days. He asked me if I thought I could beat that time. Presented that way, it felt like a competitive event. It became my challenge point. And I thrive on a challenge."

"What was your original goal?"

"I first thought I would try to cross the country in thirty days," he answered, then added, "I put myself through a twenty-four hour trial to see how far I could go in twenty-four hours. I needed to convince myself that I could go the kind of hours I needed to go, that I could cycle all day and all night if I had to."

"And how did that trial go?" I asked.

"Well enough to inspire me to increase the goal. I began to brag that I could do it in twenty-five days.

Then I boasted I could do it in twenty-one days. That's when people started laughing. They pointed out that I could inflict chronic damage to my arms and shoulders from such abuse. So I went back to my goal of twenty-five days.

"I left Orange County on August 26. I cycled for forty hours without any sleep. I awoke the next morning and my arms felt useless, like two big pieces of meat hanging there. It took three or four hours to warm them up. But each day it got easier and easier. I slept about four and a half hours a night on this trip. We arrived in New York City, eighteen days, sixteen hours, and fifty minutes after we started!"

"Wow! You did it!" I exclaimed. "You did it in almost half the time Bob Whelan first did it."

"Yes."

"In fact," I added, "You OUTDID it."

"Yes."

I can't tell you how this man, David, inspires me. He is living testimony to the power of goals and the power of following a leader who wants you to succeed. I asked him, "Do you still have any low times?"

"Oh, yes." He added, "Life is made up of ups and downs. And when I'm feeling down or depressed is when I am without any particular goals. A lot of times, what I do is project myself a little farther into the future. I plan positive plans and then I know it's going to get better."

Positive planning with the expectation of good from God propels him on toward his goal.

WORK POSITIVELY

When you are hit by a bitter disappointment, when you encounter a tragedy, you can be disappointed, but not defeated if you can continue to think positively, plan positively, and work positively.

THINK: "I can live through this! I can survive, even thrive through this!"

PLAN: "Now what? This is where I've come from. This is where I want to go. This is how I will get there."

WORK: Plan your work and work your plan. "I will give it all I've got and I've got more in me than I think I do."

I have seen people energized by dreams. A dream, a positive plan can recover wasted resources. There are countless minutes in the day that could be better spent if you had a plan. When you don't have a plan, the time can get away from you. Time gets lost without a schedule. That's why the old axiom still holds true, "If you want to get something done, give it to the busiest person you know."

A positive plan can unleash latent energy. When you have a plan, the excitement from working on the plan will create literally more energy than if you had no direction. Lethargy is a natural by-product of aimlessness. That's why people who get up one hour earlier to exercise, report a greater amount of energy. They are able to do more and need to sleep less. They have taken good care of their bodies and have invested wisely in body energy.

A plan gives direction.

A dream gives energy.

You'll accomplish far more than you would have if you didn't have a dream. Debbye Turner, Miss America 1989, understands this. I was so impressed when this dynamic young woman called our office and asked if she could be interviewed on the Hour of Power. She was looking for platforms which allowed her to share her positive faith. We definitely fit that criterion, and we definitely were interested in interviewing her.

As Miss America, she had given countless interviews. Debbye handles the responsibilities with all the poise, grace, and charm of a typical pageant winner. Yet she possesses strong convictions about her faith, family, and perseverance which make her an inspiring and refreshing role model. Her love of animals has led her to the profession that is her real dream and passion—becoming a veterinarian. Her dreams have become realities, but they only came after years and years of hard work.

I asked her, "Is it true, Debbye, that it took you seven and a half years to make it to the Miss America title?"

Laughing, she quickly admits, "Oh, yes! I entered the Miss America preliminaries seven and a half years before I won the Miss America title. I wanted to go into veterinary medicine, and that's an expensive education. For the first two or three years, I participated to win as much money as I could.

"Over the next year or two, I really began to believe that God had a purpose in my continuing and not giving up. I think deep down in my heart I believed I *could* win the Miss America pageant, but I didn't believe I *would*. I did know that I should not give up, that I was to continue to try until I finally won the state competition."

"How did you handle the disappointment when you didn't win?"

"Each time I didn't win it was disappointing, especially on the state level, because there was a lot of time, effort, and emotion invested. But each time I looked back and evaluated how I did: *Could I be better? Was I really ready to win?* I took those experiences and learned what else it took to be a winner.''

''What do you tell young people when you speak?''

''Do everything with excellence, whether it's homework or projects, something for the community, mowing the lawn, or washing out the bathtub. Do it in excellence. Take pride and take care in what you are doing. Never give up on your dreams.''

Remember you are surviving. You have a plan and you're working on it so that your dreams will come true.

LIVE POSITIVELY

Are you living right? There is basic morality that you need to adhere to if you want to handle disappointments successfully. My last book, *Believe in the God Who Believes in You,* is an in-depth look at the Ten Commandments. In that book I portrayed the positive aspects of the Ten Commandments. Throughout history, theologians have interpreted these ten commands as negative ''Thou Shalt Nots.'' Such a shallow discourse on these brilliant guidelines has inhibited people from discovering the freedom that comes from living God's way.

The Ten Commandments are not ten rules to keep you from having fun. They are ten disciplines that will help you to become a top achiever. When you live right you won't be disappointed. You will be happy with yourself even if you don't succeed in reaching your goal. If you live right, you'll be able to look in the mirror and be proud of the person you are. You'll have self-respect. That self-respect will help you handle any disappointment!

You can handle a disappointment as long as you are

proud of who you are. Live in such a way that you won't be ashamed of what you do.

It's never too late to discover a positive life. We've all made mistakes. Even the worst of us can start over. If you don't believe me, then believe Bill Sands. Bill's no longer living, but his wise advice lives on in his book, *My Shadow Ran Fast*. This fast-paced thriller is a real-live autobiography that describes Bill's life as a prisoner in Sing Sing. This tough inmate arrived at Sing Sing with prison records stamped, "Incorrigible—not eligible for parole."

Fortunately for Bill, the warden at Sing Sing was Warden Duffy. Warden Duffy viewed his responsibilities as opportunities. He did not view these men as people who needed to be locked up the rest of their lives. He saw them as precious souls who needed to discover their worth. He looked for good to unlock. Bill Sands' life changed one day when Warden Duffy came to visit him in his cell. He said, "Bill, how would you like it if these walls would turn to butter and they would melt? How would you like it if these steel bars were made of snow, carved of icicle and the sun could melt them and you could just walk right out of here? How would you like that?"

Bill Sands glared at the warden and growled, "Warden, you're not fair. You know that's not possible. You and I both know what's stamped on my record: 'Incorrigible—not eligible for parole.' "

But the warden was undaunted. He looked Bill squarely in the eyes and said, "I know that. But I believe people can change. And Bill, if you would dare, for the first time in your life, to let love come into your heart instead of hate, if you could let love control you instead of anger, Bill, you would be a new person. And this NEW person might be eligible for parole! And that's why I came to sit in this cell with you right here. It's your decision.''

Amazing! Once Bill felt that someone believed in him, once he caught a glimpse that his life could change, that his destination wasn't carved in stone, he was able to accept love and begin to live by faith. After hard work and believing in God and in himself, Bill was released from prison. He did a wonderful work for prisoners until he died, too young, from the ravages of the body's injuries in prison and before he got to prison. I was happy and honored that I had a chance to get to know him and learn from him while he was still alive.

If Bill Sands were here, he would tell you that if you wanted to live positively, you could start by learning to LOVE positively. And that's what Jesus said, too. When the disciples came to Him and asked Him which of the commandments were the greatest, Jesus surprised them with a new commandment. It's often called the eleventh commandment. It summarizes all of the Ten Commandments into one positive commitment. Jesus said, "Thou shalt love the Lord, thy God, with all your heart, with all your mind, and with all your strength, and you shall love your neighbor as yourself.''

Drive the negative fear, the damaging rage out of your life with positive love. It takes courage to love. It takes a brave heart that risks being broken to discover the joy of love.

Take a look at another life that lived and worked at Sing Sing. Before there was Warden Duffy, there was Warden Lowe and his wife, Catherine. Catherine was another beautiful believer in God. She believed in the God Who believes in people, Who never gives up on people.

She was dismayed to learn that the warden's wife was never allowed to go into the prison. She was just a young wife with two little children, but she had dreams, and her dreams were to bring love behind the walls of hate.

She inquired. She was informed that the law was rigid; there could be no bending of the rules. She was absolutely, totally, forbidden to enter. "How can I help out here?" she thought. Finally she decided and declared, "That rule is wrong. And if it's wrong, I will not abide by it."

When the first inmate basketball game was announced, Catherine risked harsh disciplinary action when she took her little girls and sat in the bleachers. The prisoners were amazed and intrigued by this woman who would take her children into such a hell-hole. Who was she? What was she up to?

Catherine got away with her risky entrance into the world of Sing Sing. For some reason, she was not chastised. That one step led to more, bolder steps. She was determined to make a difference. She sought out the toughest and the meanest and took them on with love and kindness.

One day she met Jack. This huge murderer was one of the toughest of the tough. He was black, a victim of harsh and cruel racial injustices. He was also blind.

Catherine felt drawn to this hardened criminal. She visited him one day and said, "Hi, Jack. I'm Catherine."

No response. The scarred, battered face stared back with icy, unseeing eyes. The bravest of the brave could not look into that face without fear. Tiny Catherine looked back into that face with love. She was undaunted by his frigid silence. She said, "What books do you read?"

That unleashed him. He spit out the words, "I'm blind, lady! I can't read!"

"Oh, but what about braille?"

A flash of hope. Silence. Then remarkable timidity, "What's braille?"

Catherine leaped at the fleeting chance, "Hasn't anybody taught you or told you about braille?"

"No."

Here was a chance for Jack. Catherine seized it. She said, "You can read with your fingers!" She stroked his tough hands and said, "Please, let me see your fingers." She touched his fingertips, and she said, "You can read with your fingertips. I'll teach you." And she did!

Then she found another convict and discovered he was a deaf mute. He could not hear or talk. She learned sign language so she could communicate to this deaf mute and teach him to communicate! She opened doors to worlds of love for one convict after another. And that love redeemed and restored the toughest of the tough, the meanest of the mean.

In Sing Sing, they called her "The Lady in whom Jesus Christ has come to live."

Then there was a terrible car accident. It was 1937. Catherine was killed. The news spread all through the prison. The prisoners gathered in the courtyard, tears flowing down their cheeks. Their Lady was killed.

The next day, the news spread that her body was now lying in state in her home, a half mile from the prison walls. The prisoners desperately wanted one last look at Catherine. They needed to have a chance to say good-bye. They needed to be able to say thank you. More than one hundred of these men gathered at the prison gate and pleaded to be allowed to see Catherine.

The warden looked at these hardened criminals, tears streaming down their cheeks. He then made a remarkable decision. He said, "O.K., men, I'll trust you." He opened the gates. He let them walk a half mile to his home. They ALL came back weeping. When the bed check was taken that night, every man was there. Each man had returned of his own free will. Their lady's love had changed them permanently.

It's never too late for anyone to live positively.

Check the Top Ten. They will keep you from going astray. But live your life by number eleven, "You shall love the LORD your God with all your heart, with all your soul, and with all your mind, . . . [and] your neighbor as yourself" (Matt. 22:37, 39).

Do you want to learn to live positively? Start by learning to LOVE positively. When you are living positively, when you are loving positively, then you will be able to look disappointment in the face without being defeated. You will be able to lose it all, without being done in. Nobody can think positively, plan positively, work positively, or live positively all by themselves. Nobody can do it alone. We all need the loving support of a family or a caring friend. Janet Evans, Dan and Dennis Hayden, Debbye Turner, Bill Sands, Catherine Lowe had one important thing in common. They all had experienced the power of positive love in their lives.

Divine love also helps. I had learned that as a college student, even earlier as a boy living at home. The survivors of the tornado in Illinois brought back my memory of a family crisis. I watched them dig through the rubble, looking for something that they could salvage, some family picture, some favorite piece of jewelry, silver, or even important papers.

My family did the same thing when our farm was blown away in a tornado. We scratched through the rubble, hoping to recover some items of value. We found very little. We found a twisted silver spoon, a Bible that belonged to my grandfather. The cover had been blown off, but most of the Scriptures remained intact with the lovely etchings. Just as we were beginning to get discouraged, my mother found part of a plastic picture that had hung on our kitchen wall. It had once had the Bible verse on it, "Keep looking to Jesus." The picture was broken in half. We found only the top half. It said simply, "Keep looking."

We thought that was very funny. We did keep looking. We found the back of the piano and many of the strings were still tight. Then we found one item that was unbroken. It was also a plaster of paris plaque that we had purchased in a religious bookstore and had hung on the wall. It was also a Bible verse: "Casting all your care upon Him, for He cares for you" (1 Peter 5:7).

Can you imagine the impression that made on a young teenager? My suitcase was still unpacked, having just come home from college for a vacation. My school papers were gone. My beloved riding horse was dead. In the midst of that disaster, we find an unbroken plaster of paris motto: "Casting all your care upon Him, for He cares for you." The message was burned into me.

I know from firsthand experience that life can be difficult. But I also know that God is good! If you believe that God will guide you and you follow Him in faith, then you will get a new dream, a new idea, a new goal. When that happens, the disappointment has turned into HIS-appointment! You're on your way to discovering that life's not fair—BUT GOD IS GOOD!

CHAPTER FOUR

When Life's Not Fair,
Turn to Prayer

When life's not fair, which way do you turn? Try prayer. Prayer is a universal practice. The human being is by nature a spiritual being. We all yearn to reach out with our souls. We all attempt to transcend our humanity through prayer. The human being was created in the image of God. We are, therefore, innately, instinctively, incurably spiritual. Even those who have had no exposure to religious philosophy or doctrine or teaching whatever still feel that natural impulse within the breast which calls them to communicate with their Creator.

So no matter what your religious background, when life's not fair, turn to prayer. It can be the key to unlocking a tremendous healing force in yourself and in others. I've seen it happen, time after time, people healed—some physically, some spiritually, all emotionally. As a pastor I have prayed with thousands and thousands of people, from presidents to peasants, from saints to professed atheists. No matter whom I prayed with, I have never failed to see the power of POSITIVE prayer. I cannot say the same about negative prayer.

There is a difference between negative prayer and positive prayer. Negative praying is akin to complaining. Positive prayer is akin to FAITH!

The Bible substantiates this, "But without faith it is impossible to please Him, for he who comes to God must believe that He is, and that He is a rewarder of those who diligently seek Him" (Heb. 11:6).

If you want to discover the power of prayer, you will need to understand how this positive prayer works. There are six steps that define the miracle-working power of positive prayer. And when life's not fair, when hurts abound, you need a miracle.

STEP 1: "I BELIEVE!"

As a young boy I often walked the pastures of Iowa, looking for a favored old tree stump. Planting my feet firmly on the weathered wooden platform, I would stretch my arms to the blue sky and begin to preach. My words rang out in empty country hills, where cows placidly grazed. Occasionally, I would have to adjust the strap on my tattered overalls, knowing someday I would trade in the overalls for a clerical robe, a wooden stump for a polished pulpit, an empty field for a glorious church. I was going to be a minister. I knew it! I believed it with all my heart!

That childish dream grew into a prayer. I believed that I could be a minister. Even though I was a poor country boy, I would find a way to get the education I needed to become a minister of God. Everyone knew the educational course that was required to be ordained into the clergy. A young man (for women were excluded at that time) was required to graduate from an accredited four-year college and attend a three-year seminary. Where would I get the money? Education was available only to the wealthy. My parents barely scratched an existence from the ground.

Even though I didn't know HOW I would get to college or how I would pay for it, I knew that God would show me the way. So I prayed every night. "Please help me to be a minister when I grow up."

I waited on the bare platform at the local train station. I was wearing my best pants and shirt. My trunk sat by my feet. My parents stood silently next to me. My mother wiped a few tears from her soft, rounded cheeks. She absentmindedly reached for her apron, but then realized that she had taken it off for this important moment. She said nothing. That was unusual.

Just then the ground began to growl beneath my feet. I felt it. It was the rumble of the train. The rhythm of the ground matched the rising tempo of my heart. My pulse raced with excitement and anticipation, and yes, some apprehension. This train was coming for ME! It had never come for me before.

With a hiss and a squeal, the train strained and groaned to its grinding halt. "All aboard!" This was it! This was my turn! Dad lifted the heavy trunk up to the conductor. I checked my pocket one more time. The ticket was still there. I held it out with trembling hands. The conductor took it with no acknowledgment. Somehow the importance of this moment escaped him.

I had settled into my seat and looked through the grimy windows. Mom and Dad were still there. Mom's back was turned to me. Was she crying? Would she miss me? Dad—who could tell what he was thinking? Always quiet. So few words. But Dad was the kind of man who didn't need to talk. I knew he loved me. Suddenly I felt a rush of love and gratitude for these two gentle souls. I viewed them through misty eyes—these poor farmers sacrificing so much to let me pursue my God-given dream. Were they proud of me? I hoped so.

Seven years later, I stood waiting at the back of the Ivanhoe Reformed Church in Ivanhoe, Illinois. The year was 1950. It was the day of my ordination. I had made it! Today I was being officially commissioned to do God's work. This was my dream come true. I had prayed for this day. I had believed in it—and here it was!

I was standing at the back of the church, along with my colleagues—other ministers who had been tapped to commission me. We looked resplendent in our robes. The wood trim in the polished church gleamed. The music from the organ and the choir began to swell. It was just as I had imagined it would be, years ago in the pasture.

My only sorrow was that my parents couldn't be here to share this moment with me. But they lived six hundred miles away, a long car ride away! They had given so much to help me get here. Just then the door squeaked open. It was unusual for anyone to be so late for an ordination service. Like weddings, people always came early so they wouldn't miss the processional. Naturally I looked to see who the tardy person was. Through the door hobbled an old man on a cane. His white hair and bent back wrenched at my heart. How had he gotten here? I didn't think he or Mom were coming. But here he was! My father!

There wasn't time for a greeting; a nod would have to do. I stood up as straight as I could and held my emotions in check. That isn't easy for me to do. Afterward I rushed up to him. "Dad! What a wonderful surprise! I didn't know you were coming!"

"I had to. This day was an answer to my prayers." (Dad's prayers? I had thought they were mine alone.) "I never told you I wanted you to be a minister because

I wanted it to be between you and God. I never wanted to think you had done this for me. But now that you've made it, I have to tell you. When your mother discovered that she was pregnant with another child, I prayed and asked God that it would be a son—a son who would grow up and be a man of God—a minister. I prayed every day for you, Bob.''

The prayers of a child. The prayers of a father. Prayers rooted in faith and belief.

Prayer! And belief! They go hand in hand. You can't have one without the other.

My ministry was influenced early on by the writings of a great minister, Dr. Daniel Poling. Dr. Poling was the minister who preceded Dr. Norman Vincent Peale at the Marble Collegiate Church in New York City. Dr. Poling was known and loved as a great preacher. He was a man of great faith. He was also a father.

His son served our country in World War II as a Protestant chaplain. Now, as you all are aware, our armed forces are comprised of young men and women who come from a variety of religious backgrounds. Because our country believes in freedom of religion, it is standard procedure for the military to provide religious support for people of all faiths. At the time of World War II, the three main religious groups were Protestant, Catholic, and Jewish. Each ship had a Protestant chaplain, a Catholic priest, and a Jewish rabbi on board to tend to the sailors' spiritual needs.

Daniel Poling's son served as a Protestant chaplain aboard the *Dorchester* during the war. The ship was struck by a torpedo. It was going down. The lifeboats were lowered. The sailors donned their lifejackets. The three chaplains, noticing that there were not enough jackets to go around, gave theirs to the sailors. They clasped their hands in prayer, and were last seen alive linked in heart and hand in prayer.

Dr. Dan was devastated when he heard the news that his son had drowned. It was small consolation that he had died a hero's death. As far as he was concerned, his son was gone. He had lost a lifelong friend. He grieved. God seemed very far away. Prayer became futile. Life wasn't fair—that's the truth! Good men died —and some not-so-good people lived!

One morning he woke up, ready to give up on God. He was ready to give up on faith. Then he walked to the window, looked out across the city and with all the strength he could muster he declared—out loud—"I believe! I believe! I believe!"

Nothing changed. His heart was still broken. God still felt distant. But the next morning he prayed the same prayer, "I believe! I believe! I believe!"

So it went, day after day, those two words repeated over and over again, until one morning he woke up and realized that he *did* believe. He knew God was alive and that God loved him and loved his son. God's love broke through. Faith was reborn. Life was rekindled.

Those two words, *"I BELIEVE,"* can make the difference between sinking and swimming. They can make the difference between surrendering or surviving. They can make the difference between life or death.

Do you pray? Have you ever talked to God? Do you wonder if He exists? Does He care? How can He still love you?

Start each day with these two words. Go someplace where you don't have to worry about feeling foolish. Then look out the window and say them, however tentatively, "I believe! I believe! I believe!"

Don't expect fireworks. They don't go off the first time. Or the second. Or the third. But keep it up. Keep affirming the fact that you believe! You believe in God! You believe in yourself! You believe in new tomorrows! You believe in second chances. You will be amazed at

the doors of faith that this simple exercise will open for
you.

Positive prayer starts with two life-changing words—
"I BELIEVE!"

Step 2—"I Need Help!"

You've taken the first step. You've opened the windows of faith. You believe that God can help you, but
you've been afraid to ask him. It feels selfish to pray for
yourself.

Go ahead. Do it! Ask Him! He'll understand. He
knows the longings of your heart. The Bible tells us
"Yet you do not have because you do not ask" (James
4:2). The truth is, many so-called selfish prayers are
very humble prayers. Some of you will never find the
power breakthrough you need until you dare to be
"selfish" in your prayers, until you are able to say,
"God, I need help! I can't do it alone."

In Alcoholics Anonymous they wait until the alcoholic hits rock bottom. When he is in the pits, he has
enough authentic humility to say, "I need help! It's out
of control."

That's petition. The Bible says, "Call to me, and I
will answer you, and show you great and mighty things,
which you do not know." (Jer. 33:3).

You have needs that must be prayed for: In your
marriage, in your business, in your studies, at school, in
relationships. God wants to help you. He wants to be
your best friend.

The Bible makes it perfectly clear: "Ask, and it will
be given to you; . . . (Matt. 7:7). Ask! Let God help
you. Many of you are never going to get your life together until you become humble enough to say, "I
need help, Lord! I can't do it alone."

Baseball star Steve Howe used to pitch for the

Dodgers. In 1980 he was the National League's Rookie of the Year. He was a World Series winner in 1981 and an All-Star player in 1982.

Then all of the success, all of the glory came crashing down as the world discovered that Steve was addicted to cocaine and alcohol. His addiction was real. One recovery program after another failed. The world watched as Steve returned to the mound after "graduating" from each of these programs, only to hear the news soon after that Steve was using again. The Dodgers were patient with Steve, but eventually they had to give up on him. They let him go his own way.

Another prominent team picked him up after he went through another clinic. They offered him a six-figure bonus if he could remain drug-free. But the pull of the drugs was stronger than any clinic; it was more powerful than monetary incentives; it even outweighed fear of death or prison.

I asked Steve how it was that drugs and alcohol could have such a devastating impact on his life. Here's what he said:

"I started drinking when I was fifteen years old. I drank to medicate the way that I felt and to take away feelings that I had about myself."

"What were those negative feelings?"

"Basically I didn't care whether I lived or died. I was afraid to live, yet I was afraid to die. I was in a state of no return, and I didn't know how to get out of it. I didn't have any hope."

"Is it true that several of your friends were killed as a result of drug use?"

"Yes. Nine out of fifteen of my close friends are dead. Every person that I've lost has died as a result of drugs and alcohol. Car accidents. Getting shot. Hit by a drunk driver."

Nothing was able to save Steve from his destructive

spiral. The fearsome journey is chronicled in a book, *Between the Lines: One Athlete's Struggle to Escape the Nightmare of Addiction* (Masters Press). In December 1988, after Steve finally hit rock bottom, God moved in to pick up the pieces that his life had become.

"I'd just gotten out of another rehabilitation center," Howe recalled, "and some friends, my pastor, and a pastor I had just met from another church came over. I didn't know what to do. I had tried everything else. I'd had the best psychologist, the best psychiatrist, the best treatment centers that money could buy," he said, "But until I got down on my knees and asked for forgiveness and gave the Lord all my heart . . . I didn't have a chance."

Now, after nineteen months of complete abstinence from alcohol and cocaine use, Steve Howe has returned to baseball. In fact, Steve is currently pitching for the New York Yankees. Listen to Steve's testimony:

"Only by the grace of God have I been able to turn my life around and still have many things intact," Howe said. "The only thing I need is God. He is stronger than any alcohol support group. Romans Chapter 8 says that but by the grace of God—you know, He sent Jesus to die for us so that we may live. When I read that I said, 'Amen!' "

Steve prayed those miracle-working words, "I NEED HELP!"

We all need help at one time or another, so don't be too proud to ask for it when your time comes.

God knows your deepest need. He knows your deepest sorrow. He knows your secret longing and your buried fear. His shoulders are big enough to carry the weight of the world. Tap into prayer for God's miracle-working power. It's the most exciting way to live!

STEP 3—"THANK YOU, GOD!"

God is good! Yes, He is! No matter what has happened, God is there for you. And as hard and as crazy as it may sound, when the walls collapse and the world tumbles in, and when it looks like everything that we've loved is lost, that's the time to say, "Thank You, God!"

I can hear you cringe as you read these words. "Oh! That's too hard to do. You don't know what I've lost! How can I possibly thank God? I don't want to thank Him. I want to argue with Him. I want Him to put things back the way they were."

Of course you want God to repair the damage that has destroyed your life. You want your job back. You want your money back. You want your loved one back. You want your health back. Believe me—that's the time when you need most to say, "THANK YOU, GOD."

"But Dr. Schuller," you say, "I've lost everything and everyone I've ever loved."

Can you be grateful even when you've lost a loved one in death?

"That's going too far," you say. "That's expecting too much."

Yes, it is! No one says THANK YOU when they've buried a loved one. No one!

Right? Wrong! Try this—others have:

"Thank You, God, that we had wonderful years anyway."

"Thank You, God, that our memories live with lots of loving thoughts."

"Thank You, God, that I am not alone—I still have loved ones left."

"Thank You, God, that my precious one is not lost

—I know where this precious one is right now—
with Christ who died very young too."

Yes, it hurts to say good-bye forever! And when
you're hurt you want to fight. You want to punch someone's lights out. It would feel so good to let all that
hurt and anger out! So what do you do? When you
grieve, what do you do?

I have a good friend, Stew Leonard. Stew is one of
the most successful retail businessmen in the United
States of America. In fact, he has been featured in the
book, *In Search of Excellence*. And recently his dairy mar-
ket was chosen as the business that satisfied customers
more than any other.

Stew and I share a lot in common. One is a belief in
possibility thinking. Another is a commitment to our
church and to our faith. Plus we both have placed a
high priority on our family life. We are very much in
love with our wives, and enjoy the companionship of
our children and our grandchildren.

Stew has a son named Stew II. He also had a grandson named Stew Leonard III. I say *had* because the
little boy, twenty-one months old, drowned at Christmas time. How could Stew and his son and daughter-
in-law thank God when their precious little boy was
dead—gone forever?

I have asked them for permission to reprint a letter
that they sent me shortly after Stewie's funeral. It answers the question better than I ever could. It was a
brief note of thanks for the prayers I had prayed for
them as well as a copy of the program that was handed
out at the funeral. On the program was a poem that
Stewie's dad wrote, along with his mother, Kim. It
reads:

Some loving thoughts from his parents, Kim and
Stew.

Every night at two, or maybe it was three,
I would feel our little buddy, Stewie, climb in bed
with me.

Toughest part of any day
Was I'd leave for work, Bye-bye, Stewie, I'd say.

He'd stand with his runny nose pressed against the
glass.
I'd blow him a kiss; he'd do the same; another day
would pass.

And Kim would spend her day with her little pals.
Blake and Stew.
Loved to go to the dairy just to hear the cows go
Moooo.

When we got home at night, would load 'em in the
jeep,
Drive and drive and drive till he fell asleep.

Although these things have changed, we've learned
with the help of families and friends,
Every life has a beginning, but never an end.

Kim and I believe things will be all right.
In our memory, little Stew will still be sleeping with
us many a night.

Our marriage is strong, it's been put to the test.
We know that things somehow will work out for the
best.

We remember how Stewie climbed up a slide, came
down flat on his back.

We'd say, Stewie, go try it again—take another whack.

He'd lift his chin and get that real determined look in his eye, then he'd waddle on his way.
Down the slide he'd come, smile so proud, because on the second try it went just his way.

If our little Stewie could talk to us now, I know you'd hear him say, Mom, Dadda, Blake, don't forget
What you taught me on the slide. Please, go on with your life; take another whack.

I've been greeted by Jesus; I'm in Heaven now. I'll always cherish the twenty-one months I had with you. But please keep your faith, and please don't change. I know I'll always be in your hearts.

Love always, your son, Stewie."

When you lose a loved one, there is a way to thank God. You can thank Him for the promise of life eternal. You can thank Him for the assurance that some day you will be reunited with the one you've lost.

The worse the loss, the harder the fall, the deeper the pain—the more you need to say, "Thank You, Lord!"

Thank You, Lord! is the force that draws back the curtains, letting the light pierce the darkness.

Thank You, Lord! is the first slippery step back up from the well of depression.

Thank You, Lord! is the seed of faith planted in the dry, cracked earth.

When you least feel like doing it—say Thank You, Lord!

You don't say thank You to God because you are crediting or blaming Him for your heartache. NO! Nothing could be further from the truth! God is good! He is the father of love and goodness! Most of the time we make our own heartache. Why then do we say thank You, Lord, in the midst of the raging storm?

We say Thank You, Lord, that You're still there to help us!

Thank You, Lord, that I'm not totally alone!

Thank You, Lord, for the help You will send me.

Thank You, Lord,

Thank You! Thank You! Thank You! It's a vital element of positive prayer.

STEP 4—"HELP OTHERS, LORD!"

The first step launches us on our journey of faith. We reach out in trust and simply say, "I BELIEVE!"

The second step is one of humility, of saying "I NEED HELP." The third step is that of gratitude, which says, "THANK YOU, LORD!"

Now, we are ready for intercessory prayer—praying for others. Our focus now shifts from ourselves.

This is a very exciting level of prayer. It is an adventurous arena where it's possible to see miracles happen. People who record their intercessory prayers in a prayer notebook and then go back months and years later are always amazed at the answers that they have seen.

"God moves in a mysterious way, / His wonders to perform; . . ." People who participate in praying for others are always surprised at HOW God has answered their prayers.

My grandsons are active participants in intercessory prayer. Every night before they go to bed, they go through their list of people that they regularly pray for.

The list gets longer and longer because they take this task seriously. No wonder! Time after time they have seen God answer their prayers of childlike faith. Right now their list includes a young boy who has a serious heart condition, complicated by a hole in his heart.

They pray for a mother who has a serious, life-threatening form of cancer. They pray for a little girl whose mother died last month. She cries herself to sleep at night. The boys are praying for Sarah and her tears. They are also praying for a little boy who has been having seizures. The doctors are still running tests. Meanwhile four little boys pray for him every night.

God hears these prayers. The grandmother of the little boy with the heart condition was touched by the fact that four little boys were praying every night for her grandson. She sent the boys thank-you notes. Then last month she called with news. The doctors said the hole in her grandson's heart was closing. There was no medical explanation for it. The boys knew right away why the hole was closing. They said, "It's because we've been praying for him!"

Last week we learned that Sarah had gotten a new mother. Sarah's dad had met a woman at church whose husband had deserted her. They fell in love and got married. Once again, God heard the prayers of four little boys.

I believe in miracles! In more than forty years as an ordained minister, I have prayed at countless hospital beds, before surgery, after surgery. I have prayed at funerals. I have seen the touch of God come into a human life.

STEP 5—"I'M LISTENING, LORD."

God wants to talk to you. Are you listening to what He has to say?

Have you taken the time recently to draw close to God alone?

Close the door. Wait for Him to speak to you. Become a feather in the wind, a leaf on the wave, a cloud in front of the breeze. God is the wind; He is the wave; He is the breeze. All you need to do is relax; let Him do all the work. He will carry you like a gentle breeze; He will guide you like a strong current. He will give you new thoughts, new insights that are the breakthroughs you needed.

In meditation, we stand before Him like a chunk of clay. We recognize that He is the master potter. We are willing to let Him do the molding. Our job is to stay put on the potter's wheel. In His good and gentle hands, He can mold our lives into something useful, something beautiful. After all, we tried to do it ourselves and made a pretty big mess of things.

God wants to talk to you. He has things to say that you need to hear. But we get so preoccupied with our list of things to do, we let our distractions blind us to His presence. His voice is drowned out by the din of the busy work-a-day world we whirl through. Sometimes it takes a tragedy or a disaster to get our attention. Sometimes it takes a disappointment or an injustice to pull us out of our dizzy, spell-binding schedule to turn our eyes up to Him, and to open our hearts to what He longs to tell us. At least that is what Jerry Levin will tell you. He said, "God cared enough about me to hold me captive long enough to pay attention to what He had to say to me."

Those are strong words, especially when you consider that they come from a former Cable News Net-

work bureau chief and correspondent. If you followed
the hostage situation in Lebanon then you know who
Jerry Levin is. He was the first American taken hostage
in Beirut, on March 7, 1984.

Jerry's wife, Sis, was with him in Beirut. When she
showed up at his office, the staff members asked her
where Jerry was. He had been late for a meeting. Nobody is ever late in television work. Besides Jerry had a
penchant for punctuality. Sis instinctively knew that
something was wrong. The word *kidnapped* surfaced immediately. Jerry had been kidnapped!

I had a chance to meet Jerry and Sis and I was so
impressed with their faith and their commitment to
promote peace. They had sent me a copy of Sis's account of the hostage situation as they experienced it
first-hand. The book is entitled, *Beirut Diary.* From an
educational perspective, the book is the clearest statement on the Middle East situation that I have read.
Through her eyes I learned more and understood
some of the complicated issues as I had never before.
As the wife of a kidnapped journalist who came onto
the scene with little prior knowledge of the Middle
East situation, Sis was forced to untangle the confusing
web of political and religious concerns.

Talk about an injustice, a disaster! Imagine Sis's situation. Her loved one, her best friend, Jerry, had been
taken captive. Was he dead or alive? Would she ever see
him again? Would he ever be released? What a helpless
feeling for a small American southern Christian con-
servative woman, married to a Yankee Jew assigned to
cover a predominantly Muslim country. She was a foreigner in a strange, hostile country. Alone.

Meanwhile, consider Jerry's perspective. One day
he was walking along the street of bustling Beirut. Suddenly he's thrown into the back seat of a car. A blind-
fold is roughly tied over his eyes. There is no question.

He is being kidnapped. By whom? Will they kill him? Or is he to be held for barter power? Where is Sis? How will she handle it when she hears the news? Will he ever see her again?

When Jerry was taken hostage, he was a self-proclaimed atheist. He was born and raised in a Jewish home, but he had discarded all remnants of faith in a personal God. Alone in a cell, chained to the wall by the wrist and sometimes ankle, too, blindfolded continuously, Jerry had only his mind, his keen intellect to keep him company. So he began an intellectual journey, which then became an emotional journey and then a spiritual journey. Very few days had gone by before he felt an almost irresistible urge to talk to himself. As he said to me, "I felt I had to hear the sound of my voice, but I didn't want to talk out loud because I was afraid I'd go crazy."

One day it occurred to him that people had been talking out loud for centuries to this thing called God. People had done this for thousands of years and they hadn't gone crazy. That's when he thought, *Maybe I can do that too.* That started him on his inward journey to faith—that finally led to a point where he simply believed.

At that moment of belief and acceptance of both God and His Son, Jerry prayed his very first prayer. He asked God to protect his wife and children. In addition he said, "It was very clear to me that I had to ask Him to forgive my captors."

Now, while God was speaking to Jerry's heart, Sis was spreading seeds of love and peace in the Middle East. She had returned to the Middle East in an attempt to negotiate Jerry's release. While waiting and seeking out opportunities to talk to the people who might be able to help, Sis had spent her spare time working with the hurting children of Syria. She had discovered that there were numerous children who had been left homeless, destitute, crippled by the war.

Sis had been raised in a Christian home. She had always had a strong relationship with Jesus. So when the ambassador asked her to preach in the church in Damascus, she gladly responded affirmatively. In her message at the Damascene church she talked about forgiveness. That was a real surprise for a people who knew her to be a victim of terrorists. Sis explained that there is another way—it's called mercy and mercy meets justice at the cross.

Nine months had passed. It was Christmas Eve. Jerry was completely ignorant as to what was happening around him. His captors only told him two things. The American embassy had been bombed in Beirut. A few months later, on Christmas Eve, another told him that his wife had been there. Jerry thought they meant Lebanon, but once he reached freedom, he realized that his captor meant Damascus. The man said, "She had been here talking about new ways of achieving peace and asking about you at the press."

Interestingly Jerry's treatment improved somewhat at that time, just enough to make a difference in his ability to survive disease and illness. Then they asked him if he wanted a gift.

Jerry said, "Yes! I'd like a Bible." It had been about nine months since he had stepped out on faith and had started talking to God. He had tried to recall all that he remembered about the Bible, which was very little, because he had never read one. So he asked his captors for one.

The man said, "We'll see what we can do."

Two days later they brought Jerry a little red pocket Gideon New Testament, Psalms, and Proverbs. They said, "We're sorry, this is all we can find."

Eagerly Jerry read that little Bible. In reading the

THANK
YOU,
LORD!

That You're
Still There To
Help Me!

Gospels which relate the story of Christ, Jerry was amazed by what he learned about prayer in Mark 11:24. He read, 'Whatever you ask in prayer, believe you have received it and it will be yours!' *Have received!* Past tense. Fait Accompli. At that moment he realized that despite the chains, the locked doors and guards with guns—he was free! Life's not fair—but God is good!

Of course, if you read the newspapers and followed Jerry's story at all, you know how this story ended. Happily, he was reunited with his wife in Frankfurt. Naturally, Jerry couldn't wait to tell her of the faith he had found during his months of captivity.

Today Jerry and Sis Levin travel extensively and lecture colleges and universities. In early 1991, he became director of News and Information Services for World Vision. And Sis recently received her Doctorate in International Education from Columbia University Teachers College. Remarkably, her dissertation was titled, "The Role of Forgiveness in Conflict Resolution." Jerry is quick to point out that his escape was based on faith, unquestioning faith, reconciliation and love. He adds, "Without those three things, without us all really giving absolute devoted obedience to those concepts, I think that the horrible situation in the Middle East will continue and also all hatred and all the violence in the world is going to continue as well."

I asked him, "What can we do for the rest of the hostages?"

"I think that we have to pray very, very hard—for both our President and the leaders of Iran who quite clearly have a great deal of control and influence in this situation. They are the ones who are going to have to find some way of reaching an accommodation. And I think we have to pray very hard that they maintain or acquire those characteristics and traits of the soul that will help them to deal with each other about this problem in a manner that Jesus taught."

God waits every day for you and for me to stop for a moment and listen to Him. What an honor to think that the Lord of the universe has things that He wants to tell YOU! When was the last time you talked to Him? When was the last time He talked to you?

You say He's never talked to you? Well, maybe that's because you weren't listening. Or maybe it's because His voice was drowned out by traffic, by telephones ringing, by the rush of the calendar. God's voice is a still small voice. It will come as a positive idea "out of the blue"—or as a positive "feel-good feeling"—or as a pleasant memory coming to your mind—or as an unexpected visit from someone.

If you want to hear Him, you have to seek Him out in a quiet, all-alone kind of spot. Even Jesus withdrew to hear His Father's voice. Time and time again it tells in the Bible how Jesus retreated to a solitary place to pray. Christ's method of praying was so different from the rabbis and teachers of his day. In first-century Judaism, prayer was most often done by priests and high holy men openly in the Temple. They stood on the Temple stairs, bowing and praying dramatically. The older the priest and the longer his shawl, the holier the individual. Prayer was a religious ritual to be repeated. To Jesus, prayer was a relationship to be experienced!

Every day at noon, the Sanhedrin, consisting of the Pharisees and Sadducees, met for afternoon prayer. Their prayer rituals were intense. Each member held a phylactery, a three-inch-square black wooden box. Inscribed on the surface of the box was the name of God. Inside were the four sacred passages from the Torah. Attached to the phylactery were long leather straps. During the prayers, the priests wrapped these straps around their arms. Their chants in Hebrew could be heard throughout the Temple area.

In contrast, Jesus prayed alone, in secret. He would often retreat to the mountains or to a boat in the middle of the sea. His prayers were simple conversation and communication with His best friend—His Father! He lived out the principles of prayer as He outlined them in the Sermon on the Mount. He said,

> And when you pray, you shall not be like the hypocrites. For they love to pray standing in the synagogues and on the corners of the streets, that they may be seen by men. Assuredly, I say to you, they have their reward. But you, when you pray, go into your room, and when you have shut your door, pray to your Father who is in the secret place; and your Father who sees in secret will reward you openly. But when you pray, do not use vain repetitions as the heathen do. For they think that they will be heard for their many words. Therefore do not be like them. For your Father knows the things you have need of before you ask Him. (Matt. 6:5–8)

If Jesus, God's Son, needed to withdraw to hear God's voice, don't you think that the same might be true for you? "God knows the things you have need of." How can you ask for something you don't even know you need? God knows what it is you need. Ask Him. He will tell you.

His voice may come in the form of an idea. It might come in the mail, a letter from someone who cares and gives you the courage to go on. God's voice can be heard through phone calls—from an old friend, a family member, "I was thinking about you today." You can hear God's voice when you read the Bible. Sometimes

He even speaks through ministers or inspirational books.

You can hear God. He will talk to you—indeed He has talked to you—chances are you just didn't recognize His voice when He spoke. Open your eyes. You will see God at work in your life. Open your ears. You will hear God's voice.

LEVEL 6: "USE ME, LORD."

How do you want to be remembered? All of us think about it from time to time. I would hope that after I have died, that people would say of me, "He was an encourager." I want to encourage people, give them hope and courage. I want to be a blessing.

Anybody can be a blessing. You only need three things: A head, a heart, and hands. You only need to be able to give a look, a word, a touch. Anyone can be a channel of a blessing.

God needs you. He wants to use YOU! Prayer is much more than a cloistered life. Prayer is living out God's words. It is putting faith into action. It is a mind through which God is allowed to think. It is a heart through which God is allowed to love others. It is eyes that see, deep, beyond into the soul of people—into their hurt, their pain, their suffering, their disappointment, their discouragement, their worries and their sin.

Prayer is more than words. It is a look, a word, a touch.

When you say, "Use me, Lord," you are really asking for it! God never turns down such a generous offer. And when He begins to work in your life, you had better hold onto your hat, for it's never boring when God uses you. You don't have to take my words for it. Bruce Olson will tell you—his life has been one exciting moment after another since he prayed, "Lord, use me."

Bruce was only nineteen years old when he left the United States for Venezuela and Colombia. Bruce is a modern-day missionary. His story has been told in *Reader's Digest* as well as other magazines. I heard about his remarkable work and wrote to him in Colombia. I was not sure what kind of mail system they had there, but much to my surprise, I got a letter from him saying he was coming back to the United States in a few weeks. Would we be able to meet then? Absolutely!

Three weeks later I met with one of the most remarkable men living today. If you think Indiana Jones is an exciting character, wait until you meet Bruce Olson.

Bruce was a gifted linguistics student. He decided to use his gifts of language to teach primitive people living in the jungles of Colombia about the love of Jesus. Bruce had heard that the Motilone Indians were dying. They were being killed by disease. This tribe of people are one of the very few people who still live in the stone age. They are very hostile. They have successfully warred against the Western world. Even Shell Oil Company had been unable to penetrate their midst.

When I met this quiet, bookish man, I said, "Bruce, tell me, what made you think that you could become friends with these people when everyone else had been run off or killed by them?"

Bruce replied, "I was very naive. I walked into the jungles with guides. On the eighth day we felt the absence of monkeys following behind us in the jungles. We felt the absence of the parrots that accompany anyone adventuring through jungle areas. My guide said, 'We are being observed.' Five minutes later we were ambushed by the Motilone Indians. Arrows five and a half feet long came jutting through the jungle forests.

My guides dropped their bows and arrows, literally running into the denser jungles, slipping through it like deer. I ran behind them. They were my guides. I was feeling disappointed with myself because I believed that contact would be made with the Motilones. Suddenly I got tangled in a vine, fell to the jungle floor, and an arrow slashed through my leg.

"I looked up into the face of Motilones—the same Motilone Indians who had shot over five hundred oil company employees, who had resisted the penetration, the penetration of their territories by the Western world. Fifteen Indians stood over me with their bows and arrows drawn taut and aimed at me. I spoke to them in the Yuko language. I said, 'I come from afar. I want to be your friend.' They didn't understand the Yuko language. I spoke Spanish. They don't understand Spanish. So I spoke to them in Latin.

"The Motilones thought the whole world speaks their language. Their idea of life is speech. So if you're alive you speak the Motilone language. Then, one of the warriors took the arrow out of my leg and ripped it out."

"That was your introduction to the tribe?"

"Yes."

"And you've been living with them for twenty-eight years?"

"Yes."

When Bruce came, their language had not been reduced to writing. Bruce reduced their spoken language to writing. He translated the Bible into their language and then he began to educate them in health practices, until today the Motilones have ten medical centers, twelve schools, and eighteen agricultural centers. But Bruce's work is far from over. Last year Bruce was captured and taken hostage by guerrillas.

I asked Bruce why he, of all people, had been kidnapped.

He said, "To understand why they wanted me out of the picture, you have to understand my work with the Motilones. When I asked God to use me and He responded by sending me to the Motilones, He made it clear that He wasn't calling me to pull the Motilones out of the jungles into a square church building or to teach them Western music. It was not my mission to impose Western life-styles on the Motilones. I was merely there to teach them what I knew and it was their choice to take what they wanted. So all of the work that I have done with the Motilones stays with the Motilones.

"So the Motilones produce their own nurses. They produce their teachers. They've graduated many of their students from our high schools and universities, but not one Indian has abandoned the jungles to become a Westerner. The Motilones have become a testimony in Colombia. The people of Colombia talk about them as the most primitive Indians of Colombia who are today at the vanguard of community development.

"The guerrilla organizations in the borders of Colombia with Venezuela see the dynamic of the Motilone experience and they want to bring the Indian populations, which are 150,000 people, into the movement of national liberation. The guerrillas thought that capturing the friend of the Indians—ME—would bring them into subservience and force them to join the revolution."

"So you were captured in October of 1988?"

"Yes. I was traveling with twenty Motilones when we were ambushed in an area adjacent to their jungles. The impact of the bullets hit the earth. It appeared as if the earth was literally boiling. Several Motilones were wounded. I was bound and taken into the jungles. We walked for three days to the head waters of the St. Miguel River where I was shackled to a tree for two and a half months.''

"Day and night?"

"Day and night with two guards at my side twenty-four hours a day. The base guerrillas who acted under the instructions of the national *responsables* were sympathetic towards me because they are the poor, the lower society people fighting for social causes. I saw that they didn't know how to read or write. They could sit around and discuss communistic theories, but they couldn't write their mother a short note. So I began to teach my captors. They wanted me to read Marx and Engels to them. I asked them to get me a copy of the New Testament. They complied.

"I opened to the book of Matthew and read the Beatitudes of Christ (Matt. 5:3–12), 'Blessed are the poor . . . Blessed are the meek . . . Blessed are those who hunger . . .' The guerrillas said that Christ was articulating what they wanted as social justice for Colombia. I explained that Christ did not destroy His enemies as they were doing in the revolution, but Christ recreates the heart from within, makes us a new creation and brings us into community congruency. The result of that captivity was that over sixty per cent of the guerrillas accepted Christ's position."

"You were held captive for how long?"

"Nine months."

"Were you tortured?"

"Oh, yes! Remember, my captors were members of the Radical Communist party. They kill their enemies. They torture and kill their captives. When I refused to take part in their plans, I was drowned and resuscitated. I was beaten. One beating led to internal hemorrhaging.

"When we're ill physically, often times we're low

spiritually as well and I felt in a vacuum as my body agonized. That evening as I looked up into the jungles, I saw the moon creep over the horizon. It silhouetted a tree where a mirla bird roosted. It was a miracle of God! The mirla bird, you see, is a type of mockingbird and they never sing at nighttime. But this mirla bird started singing! The Motilone language is a tonal language. They do not have to articulate words. The combination of tones bring communication and, as the mirla bird started singing, I intently listened to it and recognized that the combinations of tones and tunes of this bird were the basis of the Motilone language! Amazing!

"The mirla bird had learned Motilone tonal combinations and was singing of the experiences of these human beings! It was a beautiful presence of God ministering to my needs spiritually. I now felt the presence of the Motilones whom I hadn't seen for ten months! And in that moment I also felt the presence of Christians in the United States who had prayed for me during this difficult period!

"Four days later a *responsable* told me I would be executed. I had no reason to doubt him. After all, I had seen five people executed. Now it was my turn. I was shackled to a tree. The guns were raised and pointed at me! As the countdown began, I felt the presence and peace that only God gives in such turbulent situations. The order was given to fire. And I heard the firing of their arms and to the surprise of all the base guerrillas the *responsables* had exchanged the bullets for blanks. It was one last attempt to disarm me psychologically. The Christian guerrillas unshackled me and accompanied me to my hammock in the improvised campsite. Their warmth in Christ enveloped the whole camp. It was a tremendous experience."

"So you were saved!"

"Yes! And only a few days later I was released!"

"What was the explanation?"

"The *responsables* said that they had made a mistake capturing Bruce Olson the missionary. I didn't realize at the same time that more than five hundred thousand Indians in Colombia, speaking fifty different languages had united and came into solidarity with the Motilone people for my release. Motilone university students had been publishing articles in the national papers. Unknown to me, they had started a national movement in Colombia for the liberation of a missionary. So the guerrillas found themselves in a very unpopular stance. The only way they could reconcile themselves with Colombia was to release me."

"The story hasn't ended."

"Oh, no!"

"You're going back there."

"Yes, just as soon as I can. I want to continue to work among the Indian peoples with whom I've shared thirty years of my life. I want to share the quality of the gospel with all the cultures of the Indian peoples in Colombia. During the time of my abduction, 500,000 people speaking fifty different languages came into solidarity with the Motilones to see Christ resurrected in the jungles, to know Christ the Creator makes us whole with our Father, to share in this dynamic."

Look what happens when you ask God to use you. One man, one quiet man, is impacting an entire country, Colombia, by bringing the gentle message of a loving God to a warring tribe. The testimony of the changed lives of the Motilone Indians is reaching the world. People see and hear the difference in their lives. The message extrapolates from one man, to a tribe, to a country, to the world. Only God can do that.

Now, don't think that if you ask God to use you that you will be sent to the jungles, drowned, beaten, taken hostage, or put on the firing line. God has other exciting adventures in store for you. Life may not be always fair—but it's never dull, when you ask God to use you!

And if God uses you, will life treat you with fairness always? That I cannot promise. I cannot promise that life will always be fair but I can promise you that God will have the last word—and it will be good!

Pray—step by step—and expect a miracle. Again and again you will experience a miracle. A morning bird will sing it at midnight! But what happens when you pray for—and expect a miracle and a miracle doesn't happen?

When miracles don't happen, then what can you expect? You can expect a blessing! Life's not fair—but God is good!

CHAPTER FIVE

· ——————————————— ·

They Turned Their
OUTRAGE
Into COURAGE!

*F*ear!
Outrage!
Terror!
Unbelief!
Apprehension!
Dread!
These are all natural reactions to life's blows. None of them is a stranger. You know them by name. However, you are not alone! Others have walked in your shoes. Some have allowed the negative reactions to consume them. For them life is over, there is no tomorrow—unless they make a switch and follow the example of those who have learned to live in spite of! Others have chosen the positive route. They keep on keeping on and do the best with what they have left.

TRUE STORIES OF FRIENDS OF MINE

The men and women you will meet in this chapter were victims of life's unfairness and you'll see how they had every reason to be bitter and angry. But they all somehow managed to turn their tragedies into triumphs, their scars into stars, their RAGE into couRAGE! Meet these brave men and women and see what they can teach you.

Her Spark of Courage Ignited a Flame of Freedom

The year was 1955. The place was Montgomery, Alabama. The tiny tailor's assistant boarded a bus for her ride home after working all day. She brushed past the white passengers and the empty seats at the front of the bus. No one looked at her. No one smiled. She felt them recoil as she passed them. The white men and women sat in the front. It was forbidden—by law—for her to sit there.

She took the last remaining seat in the colored section of the bus, grateful that she didn't have to stand after working all day. However, as the bus made more stops, the empty seats at the front began to fill. All the blacks knew that once they were filled, they were expected to give up their seats to the white passengers boarding. Sure enough, two stops later, a white male boarded. The white bus driver demanded that four black passengers stand to accommodate the white passenger. He was furious when one black woman, tired of unfair treatment, remained seated. In a confrontational manner, he announced loudly that he would have her arrested if she didn't move. She calmly told him, "You may do that."

And so Rosa Parks was arrested and tried for breaking the segregation laws in the transportation system. As a result, the people of Montgomery, Alabama, protested and boycotted the bus system. Word spread, and the civil rights movement was born. Today the name Rosa Parks has become synonymous with the word *courage*. Unfortunately there is an entire generation who is unaware of Rosa's place in twentieth century history, but historians will never forget her legendary act of courage that sparked the entire civil rights movement in America.

One day I had the privilege of meeting Rosa. It was hard to believe that this tiny woman could be the spark plug behind such a momentous movement. Rosa is so frail and gentle. Her soft, kind eyes mask a steely sense of justice that ignited a nation.

I asked her, "Rosa, did you plan that simple act? Had you been thinking about it, looking for an opportunity to make your statement?"

"Oh, no. It just happened. We had endured this type of humiliation too long. It had to end sometime, and when the bus driver asked me to give up my seat, I decided that the time had come."

"Weren't you afraid of the consequences?" I asked.

"No one wants to be arrested. Yet, I was willing to face the consequences. Arrest seemed less forbidding than the prospect of living with legal separation. I was placed under arrest and escorted off the bus by two policemen. I was put in jail and charged with violating the legal segregation law in transportation in Montgomery, Alabama. When my trial came up (and of course, I was found guilty) the people of Montgomery demonstrated by remaining off the buses by the thousands. On Monday evening at the Holt Street Baptist Church, people stood in great numbers requesting Dr. Martin Luther King to lead in the boycott of the buses.

"For the next 381 days, there were many arrests made. There were some bombings and much intimidation. But the more the officials and the segregationists were determined to make us return to the buses, the more determined we were to remain off until necessary corrections were made in the way we were treated. We were a very unified people during that time. We were determined and unafraid to face whatever opposition we had to."

I asked this diminutive dynamo, "Rosa, where did you get your courage? Your faith?"

"I got it as a very small child. I was brought up to believe in freedom and equality and that God designs all His children to be free."

I was so impressed with Rosa's gentle demeanor. There was no malice, no bitterness. I asked her another question, "The theme *We Shall Overcome* was the marshall music behind the whole Civil Rights Movement. Do you remember the first time you heard that song?"

"Actually, the first time I heard the song was when I was a small child and our mother sang it. It was a little different then. It has changed over the years. The next time I heard it was during our movement in the 1950s. It has since become the theme song for all freedom loving people."

That was the truth! I had heard it, too, on the news. I said, "The whole world watched in amazement when the Berlin Wall fell. We saw on the newscasts young people marching through the streets of Eastern Europe, singing this tune, *We Shall Overcome*. When I heard that song being sung by the East Europeans, I thought of you, Rosa. It dawned on me that you started a wave of freedom that rippled round the world when you took a stand on that bus."

"That's true, Dr. Schuller. But it's not over yet. Today I am concerned about the freedoms of the contemporary youth. All of my efforts and energies are focused on helping our youth. I am hoping as we move

forward into the future, that we will be able to encourage young people to be the best that they can be
and to have courage, determination, and commitment
to freedom for all people regardless of race."

Here is a woman who had every right to be angry
and bitter. Instead of shriveling in the face of injustice,
she stood up to it. She did not militate, she merely
made a statement. She took a stand. She said, "It is not
right to treat people this way." Her courage ignited the
courage of others and still others.

Silent Victory

I first heard about Charlie Wedemeyer when I saw
him on the evening news. "Victory for Los Gatos High
School—State Champions in Football." It was a year
before I got the whole story. A movie made for television aired, entitled, *Silent Victory*. I'll never forget the
scene where the new, idealistic coach strode in front of
the football players. He looked over his rag tag team
and silently scribbled three words on the chalk board:
PRIDE and HEART!

You got the idea right away that this coach wanted
to win. He had big dreams for this team of losers. Their
losing days were over, and he was there to make sure
they learned how to win. They ran laps. They did push-
ups. Wedemeyer's football training camp looked more
like boot camp. The kids got disgusted with the new
program and the quarterback threatened to walk out.

But Coach Wedemeyer wouldn't let him go without
a fight. He challenged the youth to a race. If the quarterback won, he could go—free—never to return to
the team. If he lost, he would be held accountable and
would stay on the team. So, there they stood at the
starting line—the cocky youth and the middle-aged

coach. If the quarterback had done his homework, he might have reconsidered the bet.

The team began to work, especially when they saw that Charlie Wedemeyer practiced what he preached. Charlie was a winner. When a winner told them they could win, they began to play with PRIDE and HEART! Los Gatos began to win games. They went to the championships. They even came close to winning the ultimate—the state championships, but it always slipped through their fingers by just a touchdown or two.

Charlie was only thirty years old, and on top of the world. He had a lovely wife, Lucy, who had been his childhood sweetheart and cheerleader at Punahua High School in Hawaii. He had two darling children, a daughter and a son. He had a great coaching job in beautiful Los Gatos. To top it all off, he was head coach —his dream come true.

Then Charlie began to have problems holding the chalk and writing on the chalk board as a math teacher in high school. Thinking it was nothing more than a pinched nerve, he went to see his doctor. He learned to his horror that it was a life-threatening disease, amyotrophic lateral sclerosis (ALS), Lou Gehrig's disease. The doctor gave Charlie one year to live, at the most three.

As Charlie's wife Lucy told me, "It was devastating, because it was hard to believe that Charlie had a terminal illness. He looked perfectly healthy, so it was very hard to believe and to accept the fact that he would die in a year or so."

Charlie added, "It was not until I was driving home that it really struck me as to what the future would mean, especially with our two young children, who were then six and nine. The thought of having to leave my family was devastating to me. I was head coach at that time. It was my first year as head coach, and I wasn't about to allow a disease to take control of my life.''

What a helpless feeling! There was no course of treatment to follow—only to stand by and watch a healthy athlete quickly deteriorate and lose control of muscles, beginning with the voluntary muscles. ALS is a degenerative disease. In lay terms, the nerves in the brain that lead down the spinal column to the voluntary muscles quit working. The voluntary muscles atrophy and shrivel up, until they are unusable.

Eventually Charlie couldn't move his legs or his arms or his hands. He was not able to breathe at all, because the muscles that help him breathe didn't work anymore. A ventilator breathed for him. He couldn't eat or swallow anymore either. But he can still feel. He has sensation.

Then their worst fears came true. Charlie stopped breathing. He was rushed to the emergency room where he was given a tracheotomy. Usually a voice box is implanted in these procedures, but since Charlie was not expected to live, he was left voiceless. He will never again make a sound.

However, his gorgeous wife, Lucy, and his intrepid nurse, Linda Peevyhouse, read Charlie's lips. They serve as his translators, as his voice box. And it was with Lucy's assistance that Charlie was able to continue coaching long after anyone had thought he could.

So Charlie returned to coaching football. He refused to give up. He returned as quickly as he could to the place he loves most—the sidelines of a football game, calling plays as head coach of a football team. And it wasn't just any team—it was a winning team! Charlie's body was shot, but his mind was as sharp as ever. He determined to return as head coach until he had led the team to state victory.

He drove onto the field in his golf cart, hooked up

to his ventilator, his beautiful wife at his side. Lucy had
always cheered and rooted for Charlie. She wasn't
about to stop now. Charlie mouthed the plays, silently.
Lucy sat at his side, interpreting his plays to the players
and assistant coaches. Charlie laughingly blames all the
losses on the fact that Lucy called the plays differently
from the way he had. But the truth of the matter is that
these two worked as one to take a team all the way to
the state championship.

On December 13, 1985, camera crews from every
network descended on San Jose, California, to capture
the excitement of what was to become the most dramatic high school football game ever played, the California Central Coast Championship Game. The
media's focus was on Coach Wedemeyer. Newscasts carried the news. They broadcast the image of this winning coach and his wife. Although he couldn't move a
muscle or utter a sound and he depended on a respira-
tor to breathe, Coach Wedemeyer called all the plays,
as he had done for the past nine years! This was his
final game as head coach. And he won!

It's hard to portray Charlie's keen competitive spirit
and his sharp sense of humor through printed words.
You really have to see him to believe him. Imagine
twinkling eyes, crinkled with smiles. Imagine a wink
here and there. Lips move. Silence. Except for the hiss
of the ventilator. Lucy bends close. She tells you,
"Charlie says, 'It's great to meet you, Dr. Schuller!'"

I ask him, "How long have you two been married?"

Charlie's lips move. Lucy interprets, "Charlie says,
'Twenty-three years!'" Charlie speaks some more.
Lucy reads, "And we still love each other!" Lucy
laughs and laughs at the joke. Charlie smiles broadly
and winks.

Charlie's lips move. His nurse, Linda Peevyhouse,

interprets this time, "Charlie says, 'I never thought I would have TWO women who could understand me.' "

Lucy adds, still interpreting for Charlie, " 'Let alone one!' "

Lucy laughs as she interprets this, realizing the joke is on her. I had not anticipated Charlie's keen sense of humor.

"Charlie, is it true that you're still doing some coaching and traveling or lecturing?"

Charlie replied through his wife, "Absolutely! In fact, I really would appreciate it if you would pray for my wife and Linda, my nurse, as they try to keep up with me!"

Charlie smiles and crinkles his eyes as he appreciates the joke he has played on his nurse and his wife. He talks some more through Lucy. "Charlie says, 'God must have a great sense of humor—sending someone like me around to share His message of hope and encouragement when I can't even speak!' "

Lucy went on to explain Charlie's exhausting schedule. "Charlie is the assistant coach on the freshman/sophomore team. He goes to practice every day. He does not miss a game. In addition, we speak at different churches, public high schools, colleges, and service groups. It's amazing where Charlie's been asked to speak."

I said, "Lucy, isn't it true that you wouldn't be able to keep up with all of these demands if it weren't for your nurse and friend, Linda?"

"Oh, yes! She is an angel from the Lord. She takes care of Charlie and me. She works incredible hours. She donates all her time to us which really is an answer to prayer. Charlie requires constant medical attention, and we simply could not afford to hire a nurse twenty-four hours a day. Linda gives hours and hours, so we only have to pay for one nurse, not two. She's been with us over four years and is still with us, which is a miracle! She has become part of the family. We thank the Lord every day for what she gives and how she helps us.''

I had one question I wanted to ask Charlie. "Charlie, do you ever pray to be healed?''

Charlie's lips moved silently. Lucy said, "Charlie says, 'I always used to pray to be healed, but now I pray that God will use me. Today I feel that God has healed me from the need to be healed.' ''

Wow! What a fabulous attitude to have! I said, "Charlie, how do you keep your faith so strong? What is the source of your encouragement?''

Charlie/Lucy said, "We spend time reading our Bibles. We pray regularly and twice a week we attend a Bible study. I even go to a men's Bible study fellowship on Monday night, which is football night!'' Lucy and I laugh. Charlie winks. He adds through Lucy's interpretation, "It's so nice to rely on prayer. For so long, I realized . . .'' Charlie frowns. Purses his brow. Lucy realizes she has made a mistake. He tries again. She watches intently, "Oh, *relied* [Charlie smiles—she got it right this time] on my own determination and courage, but it got to a point where I had stopped breathing and could no longer eat. At that point, I knew I needed a higher power to rely on, and thanks to the Lord, He showed me the way and the opportunity on that particular night in the hospital when I accepted the Lord and. . . . [Lucy frowns this time. She is not sure what Charlie is trying to say] And what? Loved it? Oh! And lifted all my worries and all my burdens upon Him. I no longer had the fear of dying, because I knew God was in total control.''

Lucy gets ready to take a break, but Charlie has more to say, "And I have to tell you, the first thing I'm going to ask God when I get to heaven is *Where's the food?!*"

Charlie Wedemeyer is one of the most effective public speakers I have ever met. Yet he cannot make a sound! Through his silence he has spoken more emphatically than anyone I have ever heard. His victories on the field are one thing. His victory over his disease has been another. Where the doctors had given him one to three years to live, he has lived now for more than fourteen years. He is going stronger than ever. I predict that Charlie and His message of courage and hope will be around a long time!

Blind Man Sees with His Heart

The year was 1934. It was early Sunday morning. The streets of Ambridge, Pennsylvania, were quiet. The church bells were already ringing, alerting the sleepy town that it was time to start out for church. The frost still glazed the roofs and the bushes. The birds were just beginning to warm up their voices. Stanley Krawczyk, twenty-one years old, was almost home. It had been a long time since he had been to bed. Two days, to be exact.

There had been work to do all night at a bakery, football games to attend, and when his friend asked him if he would drive him to a neighboring town to visit his girlfriend, Stanley readily agreed. No matter that the girlfriend didn't get off work until three A.M. No matter that by the time Stanley drove back home that it would be Sunday morning.

The quiet calm of the town stole over the weary body of the tall young man. Then, silently . . . suddenly . . . swiftly . . . his world went black—forever. He fell into such a deep sleep that he never heard the horn honking. A couple who on their way to church

were driving behind Stanley had seen his head drop
over. They honked their horn repeatedly, but watched
helplessly as his car plowed into a pole. Glass shattered
and flew through the car. The sharp, jagged daggers of
glass tore at his eyes. Stanley suddenly found himself
standing in the middle of the road, waiting for people
to come help him. He had been thrown from the car.
He couldn't see anything.

Was anybody there? Would someone help him?
Where was help? He felt blood on his face and realized
that he must have been an awful sight. He didn't realize that the people who saw him staggering in the middle of the road were stunned and paralyzed by his
gruesome appearance. Finally the couple who had
honked at him approached him. They put him in their
car and brought him to the hospital. There the doctors
took him immediately into surgery. They removed one
eye and left the other, even though they debated
whether it was worth saving.

What does a young man do when the light of his
eyes is snuffed out and extinguished forever? Well, if
he has faith and a sense of humor, as Stanley does,
then he looks for inner light, or as Stanley calls it, IN-
NER SIGHT. You find what you look for. Stanley always
enjoyed life. And this new turn of events wasn't going
to blind him to the good in life. He knew he would
find it, with or without eyesight.

He laughingly told me about a well-meaning representative of a religious organization who came to visit
him shortly after he had gotten out of the hospital. He
was sitting on the couch in his parents' home when this
visitor announced himself. Stanley found it odd that
the man's questions all were voiced at a screaming
pitch. Why was this man yelling at him? Suddenly it
dawned on him. The man assumed that because he
could not see, that he also could not hear! Stanley said,

"I resisted the urge to tease this caring visitor and say, 'I'm only blind. I lost my vision—not my hearing!' "

Because he had daylight in the remaining eye, his aunt urged him to come to Jersey City, New Jersey, where she felt there would be a doctor who could restore his sight. Stanley was dubious. He had no reason to question the prognosis of the Pittsburgh doctors. Yet he complied with his aunt's pleas. While waiting in the lobby, an eye doctor happened to pass him. He immediately went over to Stanley and asked him if he could examine his eye. Of course, Stanley agreed, so the doctor, who had his medical bag with him, examined his eye right there in the hospital lobby. He said, "You will see out of that eye again. I can fix that eye. Come see me."

The doctor was as good as his word. He operated on Stanley's eye and gave him back some partial sight enough to read and write. The Beaver County Association for the Blind received knowledge of his blindness and sent a young woman to his hometown to teach him braille.

Stan agreed to meet the teacher at the bus depot. When Phyllis stepped off the bus, Stanley fell in love at first sight. He could see enough to tell that she was beautiful and just what he wanted in a wife. He was sure that he heard God tell him, "This is the girl you're to marry."

But Stanley talked back to God (as he frequently does). He said, "Oh, no, God. She's too young!"

She looked sixteen years old. Later in the day he had a chance to ask her her age. She replied, "I'm twenty-three today. This is my birthday."

That was all the confirmation Stanley needed. He stopped arguing with God and married his "beautiful doll." It wasn't long after the wedding that Stan's sight disappeared completely. He never complained. He never said, "Why did I lose the little I had left?" Instead he declared, "How wonderful God was to give me some sight long enough to see my wife and carry memories of her with me in my heart!"

Stanley and his wife became a dynamic team in the community. Stanley's zest for fun became a driving force to bring some levity into the lives of those whose lives were dreary and depressed. He began to plan parties for the Dixmont State Hospital there in Glenfield, PA. He rounded up nearly ninety volunteers each month, hired an orchestra, and gave the patients (nearly three hundred of them) the best times of their lives.

When Dixmont closed, Stanley applied his talents to bringing fun to the children at the McGuire Home for Mentally Retarded Children. There he planned picnics with ice cream, pop machines, hot dogs, and an orchestra. All they could eat—for free! He did this for over a hundred children, with the help of nearly a hundred volunteers! In addition, he raised over $5,000 to construct a shelter for outside activities.

The Beaver Valley Geriatric Center was another organization that benefited from Stanley's talents. When he suggested the idea of parties and dances for the geriatric center, the director said, "Those are fun ideas, Stan, but most of the people here can't go to a dance. They are all wheelchair-bound."

That didn't stop Stanley. He started the first-ever wheelchair dances and carnivals, complete with booths and sponsors. Again, the food was free, the fun was all free.

People in Ambridge all know Stanley. They've all bought raffle tickets from him for his various organizations. He makes most of his sales standing on the corner. One year he sold 17,000 tickets! But as Stan is quick to point out with his customary sense of humor,

"Who could resist buying a raffle ticket from a blind man?"

He laughs as he tells about the time he was called by the American Cancer Society. They had seen his name on a list of volunteers and were wondering if he would be willing to drive some people to a Pittsburgh hospital. Obviously they didn't know Stan was blind! Most of us would have told them tartly that they had made a mistake—to call someone else. Not Stan! He called around and found a driver and for two years he and his friends drove patients to their appointments.

One day he had a heart attack. He wasn't able to do his volunteer work any more. At this time the people at the Cancer Society discovered that their reliable driver of the past two years was a blind man. Imagine how shocked they were!

Life has been full of love and meaning for Stanley Krawczyk. He can tell you one story after another of the miracles in his life. He has brought laughter and fun into lives that would have known nothing but despair if it hadn't been the sunshine Stanley brought. Not only have the patients' lives been touched, so have all the volunteers that he has ministered to over the years. Time and again, a stranger has called him or shown up at his door, saying, "How can I help? I want to do something for others. Put me to work."

After forty years of working with her husband, Phyllis died on her sixty-eighth birthday. "My wife made a difference in my life so I feel I should make a difference in someone else's life." He continues to do volunteer work.

He adds, "I count my blessings and thank God for allowing me to go blind. It was very difficult at first . . . but I wouldn't have lived the life I've lived had I not been blind. I would have gotten married and just worked all my life like everyone else. One can be blind in his eyes, but that doesn't make him blind in his heart. Besides, if I hadn't gone blind, I never would have met my wife."

From Victim to Victor

It is a well-known fact that incidents of abuse increase every day. Many of you reading this book have been victims of some sort of abuse—either child abuse, or wife abuse. Your pain is real and it constantly interferes with your happiness. You have every right to say it, "Life's not fair!" Say it out loud! Say it with conviction, because it's true! You were treated shamefully. Disgracefully. And for you it will be harder than others to say . . . "But God is good."

I have never experienced abuse. But as a pastor I have talked to many of you. I have looked in your eyes, and I have seen your pain. I hurt for you, but I cannot walk in your shoes. So meet Carolyn Koons. She knows where you're coming from. She's walked your path. If you have never heard of her or her books, I highly recommend them, particularly *Beyond Betrayal, Healing My Broken Past.*

Carolyn has shared her story with many groups in our church, the Crystal Cathedral. She has led workshops on healing memories. In addition, we have formed several support groups for victims. Life is not fair for those who have been abused . . . HOWEVER, God can heal you and make you whole again. Carolyn is one reason I make that claim.

She was only eight years old. Her mother walked into her bedroom, threw her up against the wall, and held a loaded .38 caliber gun right in her face. Her finger was on the trigger. Carolyn could see the bullets in the chamber. Her mother was screaming. She was out of control. She said, "Your dad hates you; he hates

you; he hates your guts, and one of these days he's
going to kill you."

Carolyn never doubted her mother's words for a
moment. Her father was a violent alcoholic, always out
of control. She never knew when he would walk
through the door and start to hit. She lived every day
in fear that her dad would literally try to kill her.

You can imagine what such abuse did to Carolyn.
She hated what her father was. And she loathed her
mother, who served as the town prostitute. It's no wonder that Carolyn was an out-of-control kid. At the ripe
old age of thirteen she was into drinking and vandal-
ism. She broke into people's houses, tried to burn
down churches and blow up buildings. It's likely the
police would have found her, if her parents hadn't
gone to work for the railroad, which meant that they
moved seven or eight times a year.

They had always lived in a trailer on the outskirts of
town. One day as they were driving through Minnesota,
Carolyn noticed a farmhouse. It looked so warm and
inviting. Wistfully she remarked, "Can't we get out of
this trailer and live in a house like everybody else?"

Her mother turned to her and grabbed her and
said, "Carolyn, why don't you just get out? You've been
the problem in our marriage ever since the day you
were born. Every argument we've ever had has been
over you. Get out!" And with that her parents pushed
her out of the car, left her by the side of the road in
the middle of Minnesota, and drove off.

Her life went rapidly from bad to worse. She ended
up in southern California, her life-style living up to her
reputation. A Christian lady heard about her. She
called Carolyn, who was then in the eleventh grade,
and invited her to go to church. Carolyn cursed at her
and told her she didn't want to have anything to do

with churches or adults. But this lady wouldn't give up. The lady kept calling and coming out to her house.

Finally, after continual prodding and pushing, Carolyn went to the church. Then the youth pastor joined in the crusade. He called and brought her to church when she wouldn't go by herself. As she will tell you, "I guess God knew that I needed someone to really hang in with me because I was so angry and rebellious. I didn't trust adults."

After about a month of going and running away from church, Carolyn knew deep inside that this was what she was looking for. One Sunday she went forward and asked Jesus to come into her life. And she has said time and time again, "I want to tell you, it's one of the greatest things that ever happened in my life."

I asked her once, "Carolyn, were you instantly changed?"

"Yes, I was. I felt like God literally picked me up and turned my life around! For the first time in my life I had a purpose in living. All of the same energy that I had used in such destructive ways, God now used for good. As eager as I was before to get in trouble, now I was eager to search and find out about Jesus."

It was hard to believe that the lovely young woman in her stylish suit, high heels, and earrings could possibly have been such a hellion. If I didn't know better, it would have been difficult to believe that this successful educator and administrator at a nearby college had been the juvenile delinquent she described in such horrifying detail. I said, "Carolyn, how does someone go from juvenile delinquent to college administrator? Are you as together as you look? Don't you carry emotional scars with you?"

"The simple truth of the matter is that I am not the same person I was as I grew up. That's not to say that I don't carry scars. I do. I was terrorized at times by

They Turned Their . . .

SCARS into STARS!

OUTRAGE into COURAGE!

DISAPPOINTMENT into
HIS-APPOINTMENT!

You Can Do It,
Too!

vivid, negative memories. But most of them are healed today. It took a long time though. I still have to deal with a memory as it crops up unexpectedly.

"Once I became a Christian, I tried to bury all of my past and all those memories. I kept saying, 'Heal me, God,' but I kept going on with my life externally. Everything was going well, but every once in a while something would come back and I would feel like a little kid again. All those memories, all that anger would come rushing to the surface. Not only that, my dad was still alive. He still hated me. He still wanted to see me dead. He went so far as to call the university one day and leave a message that he was coming to kill me."

It is hard to imagine a parent hating a child that much. But I kept reading report after report that substantiates the distressing truth. Even so, I could not imagine living day after day with such fear. I asked Carolyn, "What did you do when you got the message that he was coming after you?"

"I ran away from the college and I was going to hide. But then I prayed, 'I am tired of hiding. Lord, if You love me, You will take care of me.' So instead of running and hiding somewhere, I went to my condominium and I waited for my dad to come. While I was waiting for my father to show up at my door, all of the pain and all those things that all those years I tried to hide, and I had pretty successfully hidden, were suddenly right there out in the open. That's when I knew I needed Jesus, not just as my Savior, but I needed Jesus as my Healer. I needed a Great Physician who could reach down into my life and heal me."

"Did your father come?"

"I sat up all night waiting for him. The next morning I found out that he was in the hospital. He had had a stroke in the car on the way over to my apartment.

He was in and out of jail after that, until he died of alcoholic poisoning. He was an example of someone who couldn't let go of his anger. Some people hold onto their anger and bitterness and then they try to impose it on other people. My father's whole life was destroyed because he couldn't let go."

I tried to imagine the memories that Carolyn had had to deal with. They must have been heavy weights. I would have prescribed years and years of therapy in an attempt to heal those memories. But Carolyn told me that she worked through her memories without conventional therapy. Instead, she asked Jesus to help her. As she told me, "It took a lot of time and many, many moments of giving my painful memories to Jesus. I would envision Jesus holding my hand. He walked me through my painful past and poured His healing over every one of the memories. I make a choice every day to leave the past behind."

Sound too simple? Well, we've only hit the high points. For the really detailed picture get her book. Learn from someone who has been there. This courageous woman has done so much with her pain. She has turned it into a platform for teaching and speaking to thousands and thousands on the problem of abuse. She knows what it feels like to be a VICTIM. She also knows what it feels like to be VICTOR over fear and pain. There is no greater courage than hers.

Broken, but Still Blessed and Blessing Others

It was a beautiful spring night. Renee's spirits were soaring. She turned the diamond ring around and around on her finger. It had been there for all of one day. Her boyfriend had given it to her just the night before. *Mrs. Bondi will surely be easier for the students to say than Miss Lacouague,* she thought with a smile.

It had been a fairy-tale weekend. Somehow she would have to come back to earth in time for school tomorrow. Renee was the choral teacher at San Clemente High School, and she knew that her students would be all abuzz when they noticed her new ring. It would be an exciting day for everyone.

She glanced around the room of the apartment she shared with her good friends Dorothy and Jennifer. There was so much to think about. Packing. Moving. Planning the big day. There were posters, souvenirs, and programs she had acquired while traveling Europe, Japan, and Korea with the Young Americans. Then there were all the music books and multitude of teaching supplies that she had acquired from Cal State Fullerton and her six years of teaching vocal music.

Life was great! It couldn't get any better! It wasn't fair, when you thought about it. Why was she so blessed when there were so many other hurting people in the world?

She managed to get herself calmed down enough to go to bed. She tossed and turned for a while but sleep came eventually. She needed the sleep. She had worked hard putting together a musical for the high school. It had been a tremendous task. But it had been worth it. The students had come through beautifully. Now that the project was behind her she was free to relax and plan her new life as Mike's wife. With thoughts of a new life, she drifted off into much-needed sleep.

She awoke at two A.M., falling out of the foot of her bed onto her head. Was she sleepwalking? No one knows. She flipped out of bed, landing with her feet in the closet and her head up against the bed. She awoke in excruciating pain, thinking, "Where am I? What happened?" Thinking that she just wrenched her neck, she started to get up. She rolled over onto her right shoulder when another pain shot through. She rolled back and thought, "Boy, I've done it now." Although she didn't know the extent of her injury, she knew she was in big trouble.

Renee tried to call her roommate, Dorothy, whose room was upstairs. Her voice was only a whisper. Even though she was a talented singer, all her years of vocal training could not provide the voice Renee needed to call for help. But her roommate miraculously heard the whispered call. Startled, she woke up from a deep sleep and sensing that something was wrong, she went downstairs to check on Renee. She opened the door to her bedroom and there was Renee on the floor. Renee said, "I need some help; something has happened."

The paramedics came and brought her to the hospital where she was told that she had broken her neck, between the fourth and fifth cervical vertebraes. Needless to say, Renee never did get the chance to show off her new engagement ring. Instead of returning to school, she spent many long months in the hospital and in therapeutic centers learning to accept the fact that she was permanently paralyzed, a quadriplegic.

When her fiance, Mike, heard about the accident, he rushed to her side. He stood by her through it all. In addition, the community rallied around her. She had given so much to the community, and they weren't about to let her go through this alone. The school administrators discussed the issue. "Take a year's medical leave. We'll talk about your future later. Something will work out, Renee. You'll see."

Mike wouldn't let her get out of the engagement. "I'm not the woman you proposed to," she protested. "I don't know how to be a wife to you."

"I love you. I want to spend the rest of my life with you," he insisted. "Now stop trying to get out of it and start planning the wedding."

Everyone in San Juan Capistrano and San Clemente closely followed Renee's progress. They all knew how she was faring. Articles about her appeared in the newspaper. Students and parents held dinners to raise money for her overwhelming medical costs. My son, Robert, who lives in San Juan Capistrano, naturally heard about her, met her, and thought I should meet her. He told me I should interview her on our television show.

I thought the suggestion was a good one. So I called Renee and asked her to be a guest on the Hour of Power. She said, "Oh, I can't even think about it now. I recently started a new high school choir at the mission, and I'm getting ready for my wedding."

"Really? How wonderful! How about after the honeymoon?"

"Well, I don't know. I'm beginning two more choirs when we get back from the honeymoon. I don't know if I'll have time."

I couldn't believe it! This dynamic young woman was going ahead full steam. I could tell she wasn't about to let her wheelchair slow her down. In fact, her schedule was so full that she didn't have time to be a guest on my television show. Finally I explained, "Renee, I keep hearing how beautifully you've handled your accident. It's obvious that you don't need my help. But I do need yours. I'm writing a book that will help people. I think you could help me help those people by sharing with us how you've put your life together again. Do you think you could make the time for us somewhere in the future?"

She checked her calendar again. It took some doing, but we settled on a day when she could be my guest on the show. I even talked her into singing a solo. I had expected to meet a dynamic personality. That was obvious from the phone conversation. However, I was unprepared for her natural beauty. This lovely young girl had a radiant smile that lit up the room. There wasn't anything gloomy about her. Her blue eyes danced. She glowed. An inner joy flowed unchecked, like a trickling stream. You could hear it in her laughter and her enthusiastic plans for life.

She sat in her wheelchair. I sat next to her in front of the television cameras and the filled cathedral. I introduced her to the church. Then I said, "Renee! I am so impressed with what I have seen and heard about you. You're so lovely. So happy. Your life is so full. Tell me, did you get depressed or bitter when you had your accident?"

She paused a moment, searching for the right words. "Oh, yes. One day I was conducting an orchestra, dancing the jitterbug, singing, riding horses, or working with students. Less than twenty-four hours later, I was told I would never ever move anything again from my neck down."

"So you do not have any use of your arms?"

"No."

"But now you're back to teaching at San Clemente, right?"

Her eyes lit up at the thought of her teaching position. It was obvious that this girl loved her work. "The administration gave me a full year for medical leave of absence. When the year was up, they asked, 'When are you coming back?' I said, 'I don't know how I'm going to be able to do this.' But a lot of my students said, "Hey, Miss Lacouague, you always thought that we were watching your arms while you were conducting, but honestly, we mostly followed your face and your eyes. So why don't you just come back?' "

She paused before continuing, "I didn't know if I had the stamina. I also didn't know if I could handle it emotionally. I was always blessed with little successes here and there. I didn't know if I could have handled a major failure so soon."

It was hard to imagine Renee failing at anything. Her joy seemed so natural. Had she gone through the normal stages of denial, rage, acceptance, etc? I decided to ask her: "Renee, how would you describe your emotional progression after the accident? Did you ever get mad at God and blame Him for this freak accident?"

"Oh, yes! But not at first. I was raised in a very strong Catholic home. I actually felt a sense of excitement. I thought that God had picked me to be His tool, His instrument. I was sure that He was going to use me in a major way. But as time passed, as one day passed into another, as weeks turned into months, the reality and the permanence of my situation sank in.

"I could understand physically what happened to the spinal cord, the vertebrae, and paralysis. I could hear the doctors' voices and all their medical reasons why I would never move again, but I still didn't believe it had happened to ME. This happens on T.V. This happens in the soap operas. This happens everywhere else, but it does not happen to Renee.

"I kept expecting God to come through and give me back my body. But when a year had passed since my accident, I became angry. I said to Him, "Wait a minute. You've used me for a year; that's all You get! Your lease is up! Now, give me my body back."

"That's understandable." I said, "What did God say to you when you got angry at Him? Anything?"

She thought for a moment before giving me her reply. "It's hard to hear Him when you're yelling at Him," she said. "It's like yelling at your parents or your friends. You can't listen and yell at the same time. I have trouble hearing Him unless I'm completely by myself, which is not very often. As a quadriplegic, you're scared to be alone because you can't help yourself. But now, especially when I'm in bed and I'm dozing off to sleep at night, that's when I have the quiet time with God that I need."

"What is helping you to get through it?"

"That's a good question."

"I'll bet this helps," I said as I point to her wedding ring.

"Oh, yes! I suppose that most spouses, boyfriends, fiances would have walked out of my life at this time. Physically I'm not the person that Mike proposed to, but he has walked with me through the whole thing, from the beginning of getting a phone call from his father in tears saying, 'A tragic accident has happened; you need to come home; Renee's in the hospital,' to walking beside me as I rolled down the aisle for our wedding."

She paused a moment. Her eyes glistened as she recalled her husband's love for her. "You know I attend the Mission Church at the San Juan Capistrano Mission? Did you know that my pastor came to me and told me that I would always have a job directing the youth choirs there?"

"I had heard about that," I replied. "How many choirs are you directing, Renee?"

"Three—elementary, junior high, and high school."

"So God is good after all."

"Oh, yes," she said. Her eyes danced with a deep fire. "There's a hymn I love to sing that kept running through my mind during my five-month stay in the hospital. It says what I feel so much better than I ever could."

"Would you sing it for us?"

Imagine a beautiful young woman, with bright blue eyes, delicate face framed with brown curls, her arms resting lightly on the arms of her wheelchair. A clear soprano voice. Tears in the eyes. She sings from her heart:

> *I, the Lord of sea and sky,*
> *I have heard my people cry.*
> *All who dwell in dark and sin*
> *My hand will stay.*
>
> *I, the Lord of wind and flame,*
> *I will tend the poor and lame.*
> *I will set a feast for them*
> *My hand will stay.*
>
> *Here I am, Lord.*
> *Is it I, Lord?*
> *I have heard you calling in the night.*
> *I will go, Lord, if you lead me.*
> *I will hold your people in my heart.*
>
> *Here I am, Lord.*
> *Is it I, Lord?*
> *I have heard you calling in the night.*
> *I will go, Lord, if you lead me.*
> *I will hold your people in my heart.*

("Here I Am, Lord" by D. Schutte/J. Foley)

She Builds Bridges of Love—She Enables the Disabled

He was a young lawyer, a family man. He was at work when he got the call. It was the police. There had been an accident. His two oldest sons were fine, but his wife was dead and his baby was in critical condition.

Baby Peter lived, but there was damage to the brain. He was now retarded. Somehow, Dick Thornburgh managed to get through his own grief as well as be a mother to three little boys, ages two and a half, one and a half, and four months.

Dick managed on his own for three years. Then he met Ginny. She was a pretty young teacher. They fell in love and married. Ginny will tell you that Dick's wedding present to her was three boys: ages six, five, and four. She left her job as a teacher and devoted herself to being the best wife and mother she could possibly be. In time, she bore Dick a fourth son, Bill.

That was twenty-seven years ago. Today her four boys are all grown up and living fulfilling lives, even Peter. Dick has served this country as Attorney General, and Ginny has applied her energies to enhancing the country's awareness of people with disabilities. When she called and asked if I would help her open doors for the disabled, I readily agreed.

I asked Ginny to tell me how her life was changed by Peter. Here is what she told me: "When I met Peter he was four years old. He was not walking and not talking and not toilet trained. He was loved by his brothers and his dad, but was really a medically dependent child at that point. Now, I naively felt he could do more and started pushing him and pushing myself and learning about the field of mental retardation. It paid off. Today he's thirty-one years old. He is the most extraordinary man you could hope to meet. A real inspiration. Would you believe he works in a workshop? He and five other men have a small home in Harrisburg, Pennsylvania. He bowls, he roots for a baseball team. How he loves pizza. And he calls his mom and dad long distance all the time."

It was not always easy. There were many times when Ginny brought Peter to church. People asked her why she bothered to bring a mentally retarded boy to church. Their reasoning was that mental retardation prohibited children and adults from needing spiritual nourishment. It was assumed that they were unable to know God.

Of course, nothing could be further from the truth. Often it is the "simple-minded" who know God most intimately. Their childlike faith is uncluttered by the intellectual doubts that cloud the more "intelligent" minds. Their understanding is so much clearer than ours. They understand God with their hearts, when we try to grasp Him with our minds.

Ginny said, "It is because of Peter that I became involved in using my time and resources to urge the people of America to welcome those who have disabilities. Welcome them at work, and particularly welcome them at church.

"There are forty million Americans with disabilities of all kinds: mental and physical impairments, deafness, blindness. *Those people who have disabilities want to be treated as able first.* They are able to give and contribute. They do have some disabilities that need a little help, but they are able. Peter has an ability, for example, to forgive that I've not known in other people. When Peter says, 'That's all right.' He really means *that's all right.* You can count it as forgiven.

"Last Christmas Eve, Peter demonstrated his connection with God in a most miraculous way. We were sitting around the Christmas table. I decided that it would be important for us each to have a turn to speak about Christmas. I asked everybody to think about a particular Christmas that stood out in their memory. In an attempt to give Peter time to formulate his thoughts, I touched on different aspects of Christmas. I suggested that their special Christmas memory may have taken place in a particular home. It may have been centered around a special gift that was given or received. It may have been a hymn they liked, or a special decoration. After giving my big introduction I turned to Peter and said, 'Peter, what's special about Christmas for you?'

"There was a long silence. After ten or fifteen seconds Peter looked at me straight on and said simply, 'Jesus.'

"No one wanted to speak after that. No one wanted to talk about their favorite decoration or favorite gift. They all knew that what Peter had said was right and important and invaluable. He has a great ability to inspire us and keep us focused on the important things in life."

Out of Peter's influence in her life, Ginny has used her position as the wife of an attorney general to speak on behalf of those with disabilities in our country. She gives of her time and talents to promote awareness and full participation of those with disabilities. Too often we overlook a barrier. Once we have discovered the barrier, we remove it. But Ginny will tell you it's not enough to remove the barrier. It's not enough to build a ramp. You have to build a bridge of love and understanding with the Peter Thornburghs in your world. We also need to give them responsibilities. They deserve our respect and appreciation, not our pity.

Many disabled people are finding respect and love because a woman dared to give her love to a man with three boys. She opened her life to a little boy whose brain was injured. She believed in him and spotlighted his abilities. Ginny is quick to tell you that she is the one who has gained from the relationship.

It wasn't fair that a little boy was brain-damaged years ago in an automobile accident. It wasn't fair that his mother was killed. It wasn't fair that a young father was left alone with three little boys, one of them brain-damaged, BUT GOD IS GOOD! He searched high and low for the best person He could find for the job of taking on a brilliant young lawyer and his three sons. He found what He was looking for in Ginny. What a blessing she has been to Dick, to his sons, and now to the disabled in our country. As a result of knowing and loving Peter, Ginny's bridges of love are blossoming throughout the country.

Still Living, Thanks to a Positive List

Meet Joan Schabacker, dynamic educator, wife, and mother. Founder of a school for dyslexic children. One day the doctor gave her the grim news. She had a terminal illness. She had two to five years to live.

News like that comes like a punch in the gut. It knocks the wind out of you. It's tough enough during the day where the fears can be blocked out with busy schedules, but at night, as the blackness and the stillness engulf you, you look death in the face.

Joan was no different from all the other victims of terminal diseases. The nights were hell. She dreaded that time of day when she was all alone with her fears. One night as she was pacing the floors, she picked up a book that a friend had given her. It was lying unopened. Untouched. But now, with fears stealing her rest from her, she sat down and opened the book *Discover Your Possibilities*. She skimmed the table of contents. Chapter 4 grabbed her: "The bigger the problem—the bigger the miracle."

Joan had a whopper of a problem. Here was her chance to be a miracle. She read the chapter with relish. Hope began to take root in her fearful mind. Enthusiasm began to grow. Life was there—for the taking. All she had to do was reach for it. All she had to do was choose life! Positive thoughts tumbled without rhyme or reason. Joan got a piece of paper and a pencil to write down the thoughts. The thoughts began to take the form of affirmative steps. A list of positive steps grew longer and longer. When she was finished, she was surprised to see that she had composed a positive plan for survival.

This is what she wrote:

WHEN FACED WITH A HOPELESS SITUATION

PRAY—with honesty and trust in the Lord's ability to perform a miracle.

RESOLVE—the interactions which cause you anxiety and hostility.

EXPRESS—your fears and helplessness to someone you love, someone who loves you deeply.

ASK—for help and understanding, but not coddling, from those who love you.

SEEK—nurturing from your friends and loved ones —but not to the point that you will be a millstone around their necks.

TRY—to be optimistic and see and feel the good things that are happening, but don't be a Pollyanna.

REMIND YOURSELF—that God has given you a "talent" to serve others and that *only you* can utilize this talent to "light some candles" in other peoples' lives.

PROJECT—your thinking toward an event in the future (a few months away) which will definitely be a happy experience.

BUY—a new appliance or piece of furniture, or something you've always wanted, but said you couldn't afford.

CHANGE—the arrangement of one room in your house—preferably your bedroom.

INSTALL—extra lighting and windows. *Soak* in the Lord's glorious sunlight; let it pour into your rooms—especially your bedroom in the morning.

TELL—two people (at least) each day how much you appreciate them or how nice they look.

BUY—some new clothes.

WEAR—your best-looking clothes.

CLEAN OUT—the clothes you feel compelled to wear just because they're in your closet.

EAT—some fresh fruit each day.

DON'T—dawdle in bed in the morning. Get up. Get your blood circulating. You have things to do.

GIVE AWAY—a smile to two people each day!

GIVE—something away each week—even if it's small—as long as it's meaningful to the receiver.

LAUGH—once a day, find something funny! It must be somewhere!

TALK—to a friend at least once a week—one you don't see daily. Try to keep the conversation on *them!*

WRITE—notes of appreciation or condolence quickly; if you delay, you will forget to do it.

EAT—three meals a day.

DON'T—look back in anguish! You did the best you could under the circumstances you were given.

READ—a few lines from Robert Schuller.

AT THE END OF THE DAY—reward yourself by listing the nice things you did and the things you accomplished. Did you "make someone's day?"

That list was written more than seven years ago. At the time of this writing, she is still alive and working at her school. She is still choosing life and living each day according to her list.

What is your problem? Is it a terminal diagnosis? Have you lost your job? Has your company folded? Has your husband left you? Your wife? Have your children turned against you?

Whatever it is, I urge you to learn from possibility thinking experts. They did it—so can you! They felt their rage, their anger, their hurt, their pain. Some of them got mad at God for a while. But they all reached a point where they were able to get down on their knees and ask God for the ability to do the best with what they had left.

I promise you, God always honors those kinds of requests. He will always respond to a cry for help—especially a call for courage.

Make your own possibilities list. Act on the commands to eat, to give, to change—whatever. Count your assets in the face of a bleak situation.

Now, you can see why it's really true: Life's not fair —but God is good!

CHAPTER SIX

Change Your SEEING to Change Your SCENE

Life is, for the most part, the way we see it. So, when life's not fair—it may be time to check your focus. Change your seeing to change your scene. Your perception of reality will change the ever-changing shape of that reality. You have a choice! You can look at life from a negative perspective or a positive perspective.

GETTING THE RIGHT PERSPECTIVE

Artists understand the phenomenon of perspective better than those of us who do not draw. They spend a great deal of time in art school learning how to draw in one-point perspective, two-point perspective, and three-point perspective. When they have learned those fundamentals of drawing, then and only then are they able to render an accurate three-dimensional drawing of a telephone, house, car, chest of drawers, you name it. They can draw any item, from any angle—once they've learned "perspective."

You and I take perspective for granted because most of the art that we see every day is carefully, professionally executed. Pictures seen in books, magazines, and newspapers "look right." Why? Because they were sketched with the correct use of perception.

But try to draw the same picture yourself. If you, like me, have no art background, then you are probably pretty disgusted with your three-dimensional attempts at sketching. It doesn't look right. The buildings lean, the windows slant crazily. The picture is wrong. It is not a true representation of the structures.

The same can be true when dealing with life. Many of us complain high and low about the injustices we encounter. "That's not fair!" we scream silently, publicly, or through litigation papers. Many times we are right. We have not been treated fairly. But sometimes we need to admit that perhaps our perspective is skewed just slightly. We may be looking at the picture through cockeyed glasses. The one thing about perception is that it doesn't have to be off by much to give a false picture.

One of the problems with the whole matter of injustice is that it is very difficult to get an accurate rendering of the true story. Ask any judge. He'll tell you how many sides there are to a story. The simple truth of the matter is that for every justice there is an injustice. When life is fair to you, it probably is not being fair to someone else. There cannot be a winner without a loser. For everyone who gets, there is someone who goes without.

As long as you focus on what you have lost, on what you DON'T have, as long as you continue to compare and compete, you had better be prepared for the fact that there will be injustices; there will be unfairness; there will be winners and losers.

Freedom comes with cooperation. Freedom comes only in playing as a team. Freedom comes when you stop grabbing for all you can get.

Research has shown that the number one reason for being let go from a job is not inability to do the work, nor lack of competence. It is the inability to work cooperatively with colleagues. This has given rise to a new trend in education in California that is beginning to take hold. Perhaps you've seen it in your school districts as well. The concept is known as "cooperative learning."

Management analysts and educators have begun to examine the educational system for a way to teach children and re-educate adults in the fine art of cooperation. In the process, many educators have come to the conclusion that the system of grading individuals on the curve (getting better or worse grades than the other students), produces workers who fight for their place in the work field. They go out of the school and into the labor force as intelligent, hard-working, aggressive producers who are unskilled in cooperation.

Is there a better alternative? Can we develop educational systems in schools that teach children and adults how to work together? The concept is called cooperative learning. The class is divided into heterogeneous groups comprised of four to eight people, of varying degrees of abilities, interests, sex, ethnicities, and cultural backgrounds. This mixed group is then assigned a common goal. They are to research an assigned subject, discuss their findings, negotiate solutions, and present the final report as a group.

They organize themselves with a leader, a recorder, a verifier, an encourager, a reporter. They check each other's work. When two people come up with opposing results, the group negotiates and sometimes goes back to find out what the best answer or solution is.

The result is that the GROUP is accountable for finding the best solution for writing the best report. The responsibility doesn't rest on the shoulders of one individual. Because of the varied minds and backgrounds, the thoughts that are discussed are lively, stimulating, and tend to lead toward a more equitable solution than one that would have been proposed by one person's limited experience.

From an educational standpoint, the cooperative learning method has led to exciting results. Researchers report that the slow learners are learning more from their peers than they ever would have learned just from a textbook or lecture by a teacher. The other students often put the information into a language that others can understand. The top students are learning more as well. Their learning is reinforced in the process of reporting and discussing with the other students.

From a social viewpoint, the cooperative learning method teaches more than academics. Students learn more than dates and facts. They learn how to work as a team. They learn how to prepare and share. They learn how to be accountable. They learn how to contribute and how to listen.

Of course, no system is perfect. There are still weak spots that need to be ironed out when it comes to implementing this teaching method, whether it be in the classroom, the home, or the office. The exciting aspect of it is that it eliminates destructive, selfish competition. It replaces individual cut-throat tactics with helpful teamwork. There are no losers in this system, except for the ones who refuse to cooperate. Each student starts "seeing" fellow classmates as persons who can and will contribute to his successful learning. The result? He wants to help them to understand and succeed too! The class turns from secretive competitors to sharing cooperators. The "seeing" changes the scene. Perception alters our understanding of reality and eventually changes the reality itself. Your perception becomes a self-fulfilling prophecy.

If life hasn't been fair to you, then maybe you need to fix your point of perspective. Perhaps you need to look at what you can do and learn to be more than you have ever been before. Perhaps you have been focusing on yourself too much. Perhaps you need to focus on others more. Perhaps you need to learn to work as a team with your spouse, with your children, with your boss.

It's never easy to change. It is often painful. But if life feels unfair to you, be fair to yourself. Ask yourself if life is trying to teach you something about yourself. More often than not we bring about our own pain. The good news is that we can change. It is never too late to learn and to grow. There are exciting new discoveries being made every day that can help us in our quest to be all that we are meant to be.

So if the picture of your life is askew, if things don't look right, start by fixing your perspective. Look at what you can work on. You'll be amazed at what you can do and be.

Focus on What You Can Give

Get the right perspective. Frequently that starts when you focus on GIVING instead of GETTING. The picture is easiest seen through the illustration of Robert Brown, a 1990 recipient of the Horatio Alger Award.

It was my honor to introduce Robert and present him with his award. In preparing his introduction, I had the opportunity to read and study his biographical portrait. The picture that emerged was one of a generous, kind, caring man. Although he is currently a wealthy man, he learned early as a child how to keep his perspective straight. His grandmother had a lot to do with teaching him about generosity and working with his fellow man.

To say that Robert and his family were poor is an understatement. Every now and then they were lucky enough to find shoes that fit in the thrift shop. They felt fortunate to have them and if they had holes in the soles, they simply tucked a piece of cardboard in the bottom of the shoe. Clothes were also a luxury item. And sometimes food was stretched to the bare bones. But Robert's grandmother would say every day to her grandsons, "If you have enough courage, if you have enough faith in God, then you can do anything."

Robert speaks with love and respect when he talks of his grandmother. "I believed her," he says. "And I still do. In fact, I live my life by the tenth mile rule. You know that Christ encouraged us to go the second mile. I wanted to see what would happen if I went farther than that. What would happen if I went the tenth, or the twentieth, or even the hundredth? If you go as fast as you can and if you let the Lord lead you, many times there is nothing that you can't do."

"You built your philosophy and your business on the principle of honestly helping people out. Is that right?"

"It is. Again it goes back to my grandmother. Let me tell you a true story. We were sitting on the porch. I was seven or eight years old. It was summertime. This old man came by and he had on tacky clothes. He was dirty. He said to my grandmother, 'Miss Nellie, I'm hungry. I haven't had anything to eat for a couple of days and I need some food.'

"So mama said, 'Come on in.' She fed him and sent him on his way.

"I watched this tattered old guy as he wobbled down the road. Now we were poorer than most, and I couldn't understand why mama would feed men like this old guy when we didn't even have enough to eat ourselves. So I said, 'Why do you feed those people, mama? We don't have anything to eat ourselves.'

"My grandmother looked at me and said, 'Come over here, son. Sit down beside me in this chair. If I never teach you anything else, I want to teach you one thing. Life is about giving and serving and sharing. It's not about how much you get, but about how much you give.'

"I've tried to pattern my life after that."

I believe that is the reason Robert Brown has been so successful. He never forgot his grandmother's words of advice. He worked hard and looked for ways to give and share, whether it was a little or a lot. He was inspired by his grandmother to help other people. That attitude led him to starting his own business in public relations. He started out in a corner over an abandoned theater with a chair and a desk that he had borrowed from the man who owned the building. He had a telephone and a wife who stood by him and gave him active support through her multi-role as receptionist/secretary/bookkeeper. He continues to treasure her as a confidante and a continuing inspiration to him and everything he seeks to accomplish.

Today Robert's clients include such organizations as SC Johnson Wax Company, Nabisco Brands, RJR Nabisco, Inc., Woolworth Corp., Sara Lee, and others. In addition he serves on the boards of several universities. He is on the board of directors for Operation Push, with the N.A.A.C.P., and he serves on the board of trustees of his own church. He also served his country when President Nixon called him to Washington to serve in the administration. He did so with distinction and honor and was responsible for getting one billion dollars channeled for great and worthy black entrepreneurial causes and colleges.

Robert says, "It has been a great joy to me to be able to use the resources that God gave me to help someone else in these and other ways. Making money, traveling around the world, none of that gives me the charge that I get when I'm able to take what God has given me and help someone else."

I looked at this highly successful man. He became President of the railroad that his great grandfather helped to build as a slave. He is powerful and influential. He travels the world. But he is generous, kind, gentle, loving, compassionate. He views his power, his influence, and his wealth as tools to help others.

I asked him, "People could look at you and feel that it's not fair. You have so much. They have so little. They may be poor. They may be bitter. What word of advice would you give to that kind of person?"

Robert replied, "I used to wear a little pin that says, 'TRY GOD.' I would tell people who are poor and bitter to try God. Try working hard and sacrificing and having faith in God. Then you can overcome your circumstances—no matter what they are."

Bob Brown. He had every reason in the world to surrender himself to impossibility thinking. He could complain about the fact that he didn't have a father or a mother who was with him. He could complain about the fact that he lived in a house that leaked and the fact that they didn't have any money. But look what he did with the freedom to set goals. To make changes and to chart his destiny. All because of the power of God within him and the desire to help people. Look where he is today.

Question: Would Robert Brown be the happy, ful-filled, successful man that he is today if he had concen-trated on life's injustices? Would he have gotten where he is by giving in to bitterness? Or by competing against others? If his perception of reality was focused on the racism instead of upon the good qualities in persons and institutions that may or may not have been infected by racism, would he have become the great human being he is today?

The right perception led Robert to success. An-other dimension is that our perceptions of people change them! I am not what I think I am. I am not what you think I am. I am what I think you think I am! Change your "seeing" and change your "scene."

KEEP YOUR SIGHTS ON YOUR GOAL

It was that time of year. The winter chill had been chased away by the warm spring sun. The hard, dark soil had thawed. Tiny buds fringed the branches of bushes and trees, casting a hue of newborn green across the landscape. When spring came, I knew that it was time for Father to get out his plow.

It was always fun to watch Dad when he sharpened the rusty old plow on the old wheel in the workshed. Sunlight shone through the wooden slats of the work-shed, illuminating the particles of dust that swirled through the old building. Tools of all shapes and sizes were propped against the walls. Rusty tin cans held a myriad assortment of nails, screws, washers and the like. Hammers, saws, piles of wood scraps—everything was saved. The heavy scent of oily old rags filled the air.

Way back in the corner, half-buried under har-nesses, rakes, and tools, was the plow. Its rusty iron edge was dull from its winter rest. It would need to be honed before the job of plowing the fields could begin.

Dad set the edge on the old wheel and pumped the pedal with his feet. Steel ground against steel. Sparks flew. The dust of red rust billowed up. Before long the shiny metal glinted in the sunlight. It was ready for Dad to start his plowing. He would probably start tomorrow.

When Dad plowed, he was gone from early dawn to late twilight. Acres of land had to be furrowed before the seed could be planted. The tedious job could not wait. It had to be done—on time. The seed had to be planted early enough to catch the spring rains. It needed to germinate in the moist, warm, black earth.

It was my job to bring lunch out to Dad. Mom would pack up a sandwich, cookies, etc., in a tin. In addition, there was a jar of milk, drawn fresh from the milk cans. I would carry these refreshments to Dad in a pack, which I slung over my shoulder. I had to walk through the pasture, past grazing cows, over the trickling stream that meandered through the pasture, over the wooden fence, and tromp through the barren corn field, until I got to the oat field. Finally, there was Dad. Boy, would he be glad to see me!

I could see the rows that Dad had plowed. He had worked and worked. Dad had the plow in one hand and the leather straps in the other. Two of our horses pulled at the old plow. Their tails switched at the flies that had already been roused by the warming weather. The horses' hooves pounded the black soil and kicked dust back into Dad's face. He had tied a kerchief around his nose and mouth to make it easier to breathe. His tattered hat was drawn down low, shielding his head and eyes from the glare of the noon sun.

"Dad!" I called. I ran over the hard, bumpy field. "Dad! It's time for lunch!"

Dad looked up, wiped his brow. He pulled down his kerchief and gave me a great big white grin. His face was black with grit. Dad always looked so big and strong to me. His giant hands, toughened by years of hard work, were blistered in spite of the callouses. Dad rarely spoke. He was one of the quietest men I have ever known. He thanked me for the lunch, thanked the Lord, then ate.

I looked over the field that Dad had been laboring over. His rows were so nice and straight. He prided himself on neat fields. I had heard Mom compare his straight rows with those of the other farmers. She was proud of Dad. "Dad," I said, "How do you get your rows so straight? How do you keep the rows from curving and swerving? I mean, everyone knows that your rows are the straightest in the county. . . ."

Dad was a good listener. I liked to talk. Dad put down his lunch. "Come here, Bob. I'll show you." He put one of my hands on the rough handle of the plow. He put the leather straps of the horses in the other. He said, "See that stick down there?"

I squinted and tried to look past the horses. "No, Dad. I don't."

"Look for the red handkerchief. Can you see that?"

I looked again. This time I spotted the tiny red flag. I said, "Oh, yeah! I see it now."

"Keep your eye on it." Then he swatted the rumps of the horses and said briskly, "Giddyap!"

The hooves plodded and kicked. Dust billowed into my face. It stung my eyes, filled my nostrils. I blinked and blinked and managed to keep my eyes focused on the red handkerchief. It looked like a small dot. I could barely keep it in my sights. But I kept at it. Was it getting bigger? Or was it just my imagination? I rubbed my eyes on my grimy shoulder. There! That helped! Yes! The red marker was closer. Not much closer, but a little bit. I turned excitedly to Dad, "Dad, I'm doing it! Look!"

Just then the horses veered to the left, the furrow bent. Dad said quietly, but firmly, "Keep your eyes on the flag, Bob."

As I refocused my gaze on the marker, the horses straightened out their path. Dad put his hand on my shoulder. "I'll take over for now. Go on back to your mother. Thanks for the lunch."

I turned to go back to the farm house. I ran along the edge of the furrow. My feet traced the soft black mound, so straight and sure until I came to a crooked, jagged bend. This was the spot where I'd turned to look at Dad. I had taken my eyes off the marker. I then realized that the red flag was the secret to straight furrows. Success in plowing straight furrows depended on this one principle: Keep your eye on the flag and never look back! Jesus said it, "No one, having put his hand to the plow, and looking back, is fit for the kingdom of God" (Luke 9:62).

Where's your focus? Do you have a goal? Have you been tempted to look away? We are all tempted at times to be dissuaded by negative thoughts. One of the hardest facets of possibility thinking is keeping your eyes on the goal. Setting the goal is easy. Announcing it takes courage. But keeping your eyes glued to the red kerchief at the end of the furrow, when the dust is in your eyes and the sun is hot on your back is grueling. It takes hard work, perseverance, determination, and FOCUS!

I was first introduced to Sue Cleland with a story that appeared in the local paper. Sue set a goal for herself. Her goal was to win the Gold Congressional Award. This award is given to honor the men and women who distinguish themselves through unusual community service. The awardees must be between the ages of fourteen and twenty-three, and must have put in eight hundred hours of volunteer service. Sue logged 3,300 hours. Needless to say, she was given the award, along with fifty other young Americans. When she was awarded the honor, they did not know that Sue had done almost all this work in spite of the fact that she is totally deaf.

I wrote Sue a letter, commending her for her work. She responded in a note where she told me about the importance goals have in her life. I was so impressed with Sue. She could have easily said, "Life's not fair! I lost my hearing! Why should I go deaf? Why must I lose my hearing?"

Instead of focusing on the negative aspects of her loss, she refocused her attention on where she could go and what she could do, and obviously, she does a lot!—Sue's life is a testimony to possibility thinking. When she was in the eighth grade, she began to lose her hearing from systemic lupus, although it was not diagnosed until several years later. Systemic lupus is an auto-immune disease that attacks healthy tissue in the body. She also had asthma. Those infirmities later in high school prohibited her from running track and singing in the choir. But Sue wasn't about to be stopped. As she says, *"I like to find a way around obstacles so I can do what I want."*

So Sue learned how to shot-put, and in that way contributed to the track team. She couldn't sing anymore, so she chose to accompany the choir by playing the piano. She wasn't about to let little detours get her down. Perhaps Sue lives life so fully because she is glad to be alive. There was a time when the doctors didn't know if she would live through the lupus.

I asked Sue, "You are so positive. You have done so much already and you are still so young. Have you had any down moments? What were the difficult times?"

Sue said, "Sometimes people look at you differently. I haven't changed. I'm still Sue. I'm still the way I was before I was deaf, but sometimes people are not sure of how to treat you and in the process they treat you differently. The important point to remember is that everybody has a disability in some way or another. No matter what your disability, you're still a person and I'm still the same person that I was before I was deaf."

I had heard that Sue had been picked as one of only twenty-four persons to be a special ambassador for the United States at the Olympics in Seoul. I had to ask her, "How did it feel to be picked for that special position?"

"Oh, of course, it was wonderful! I had not yet been overseas. It never occurred to me that my first trip abroad would be as a representative for my country to the Olympics. The experience was enhanced by the fact that I was there as a result of participating in community service, through the Boy Scouts in particular. I was there because of programs that I believe in."

"You're at the University of North Carolina?"

"Yes. I'm studying to become a psychologist. I would like to work in mainstreaming the explorer program of the Boy Scouts of America. That way, all youth would have an opportunity to learn about different vocations. That's important to me."

"You are living a full life in spite of a life-threatening illness. You have won the top awards that this country has to offer, in spite of being totally deaf. Through all that you have thought about and dreamt about in your young life, how did faith in God fit in?"

"In high school, I was unsure what my faith was. Then, when I was in college, I got really sick. Believe it or not, my illness drew me close to God. I did not become a Christian until I was sickest, and that was when I felt God was with me. Everybody has problems

IF THE PICTURE
OF YOUR
LIFE *IS* ASKEW,

START BY FIXING
YOUR
PERSPECTIVE!

and their problems are very real to them. It's understandable that friends were drawn away by their own problems. God was the One who stuck by me every day. His Spirit came into my spirit—every day in many ways. It's a good feeling to know that He was there and is there."

Sue was able to focus on her goal. Her goal was important to her. It had meaning for her. So it drew her like a magnet. That affected her perception of reality positively! Result? Her life took positive turns! Her "seeing" shaped her "scene"!

That's what happens when God is in your goal. He gives you dreams that are important. They are meaningful. And that's the key to the drawing power of a goal. If you are starving, your goal is to put food on the table. That is the power that keeps you focused on your goal—to find food. Dad knew that if he didn't get the corn planted it would mean going hungry. His goal was important.

What is your goal? Is it God's goal for you? Does it draw you like a magnet? Does it have meaning? Will it help others who are hurting? Is anyone else doing the same thing?

If the answer to all of the above questions is YES, then you better be prepared to say NO to propositions that will distract you from your goal. Saying YES always involves saying NO. If you want to go back to school, it may mean that you will have to say NO to television. If you want to get in better physical shape, you may have to say NO to overeating. If you want to save your marriage, you may have to say NO to many distractions. Remember your goal and focus on it at all times.

Keeping your FOCUS on your goal is easier when you have someone to help you. It's not possible to do it alone. You will get tired. You will want to quit. You will get thirsty and hungry. That's why you had better make arrangements before you go to the field for someone to bring refreshments. Set aside quiet time, reflective time, refreshment time—not just for your body but for your soul. Get linked up with a positive church. That's the best place to find supportive people as well as a time and place to get in touch with your biggest support system—the God Who made you and loves you. God must be a part of your goal, the bedrock on which to build your dream and to follow your goal to fruition.

GAIN A FRESH OUTLOOK THROUGH THE ATTITUDE OF GRATITUDE

Remember a positive attitude produces a positive perception of a negative situation and eventually changes the situation for the better. The "seeing" will shape the "scene."

I only speak fluently one language—English—but whenever I am visiting a foreign country, I always learn one word and that is the word: *THANKS! Merci. Gracias. Danke. Arigato.* I have discovered that this one word alone will work wonders. It will open doors. It will establish relationships. It will be the first tender thread upon which can be woven a cable of affection and trust. Learn the power of the word *THANKS!*

Rudyard Kipling was one of those authors who was very successful in his lifetime. A British newspaper criticized him and ridiculed him and called him a mercenary. They said, "He is now writing just for the money. One word of Rudyard Kipling today is worth a hundred dollars."

Shortly after the release of the unkind article, a reporter approached Kipling at a gathering and said, "So, you're worth a hundred dollars a word. Here's a hundred dollars. Give me a word." Then he handed him a paper and pencil.

Kipling took the hundred dollars, put it in his pocket, and on the paper he wrote one word: *Thanks!*

Yes, if a disappointment causes you to slip, stumble, and slide into discouragement, then lift your mood back up by giving thanks to God ALWAYS for ALL things. Really.

My secretary twenty years ago was named Lois Wendell. She was a devoted worker in this ministry. I was home one evening when she called me. She had worked through the day, but had left early to go to the doctor. Now I heard her faltering voice at the other end of the phone. She said, "Bob, I received some bad news today. The doctor tells me I have cancer."

I could hear she was struggling to keep from crying so I said, "Hang up, Lois, I'll be right over."

I got in my car and drove to her home in West Garden Grove. She met me at the door. I walked in and said, "Let's pray." I proceeded to pray a most unusual prayer, but Lois spoke of it often, saying how much it had helped her. As she reminded me, every sentence began with a THANK YOU: "Thank You, God, that they've discovered the cancer early. Thank You that we're living in America where there are all kinds of potential treatments available. Thank You that Lois has a faith that can carry her through. And I thank You that she has a husband and children who are reinforcing her. And I thank You, God, that You are hearing and answering this prayer. Hallelujah. Amen."

Lois went on to live for many years. Eventually cancer took her life. But her positive perception lifted her spirits and undoubtedly added life to her years as well as years to her life.

Be thankful to God always for everything. I'm sixty-two years old and it still shocks me to say that I have never had anything happen in my life, including tragedies, near disasters, that did not turn out to be a blessing in disguise. I reached a point where I intuitively, instinctively, impulsively, impertinently, and I think very intelligently start my prayers with simple thanksgiving. Be thankful for all things. Exercise these nine commandments for thankful thinking. They'll help you gain a new attitude and a fresh outlook on where you can go from here.

Be sure of this: a new outlook will change the ultimate outcome. Life's unfair? It's time to practice the power of thankful thinking.

#1. Be thankful for prayers answered, known and unknown.

Discouraged? Stop! Think about all the prayers God has answered for you in the past. Some of these prayers that have been answered, are prayers that you didn't pray. Others were praying for you: friends, parents, grandparents. Maybe you sat on your grandpa or your grandma's knee and they were praying for you. Do you realize that prayers are seeds? And they can last a long, long time. One day, given the right environment, they sprout.

I remember my first trip to Cairo, Egypt. In the museum you can see kernels of wheat that were taken from King Tut's tomb. That tomb pre-dates Jesus Christ by centuries. Some of these kernels of wheat were taken out of the museum and in fact they sprouted! They are not dead! Just because they didn't sprout earlier doesn't mean they are dead. God's delays are not God's denials.

Be thankful for prayers answered: known and unknown. Be thankful for seeds that will sprout with enough patience and tender loving care.

#2. *Be thankful for sins forgiven, both public and private.*

We all have committed sins that people know about and sins that nobody knows about and may never discover, but are known only to you, your conscience and your God. So when a disappointment hits, no matter what it is, a broken relationship, a financial disaster, you can be happy if you can go to bed at night, put your head on the pillow and know God loves you and forgives you. God thinks you are fantastic! He is your best friend.

#3. *Be thankful for healings, seen and unseen.*

You can see scars. You can recall the surgery. There are known and obvious symbols of healing. But pause and think a minute, of all the hidden hurts, the unrevealed wounds, the quiet, little secret torturing memories that you carried with you and then there was that moment when you dropped them and God touched you and healed you of your hurt. You were grateful then. And you can begin to be thankful now because God won't let you down. He healed you yesterday; He will also do it today.

#4. *Be thankful for the storms of your life that have blown out, blown over, or passed you by and never touched you.*

Give thanks to God for all the narrow escapes you'll never know about. You and I will never know how often our lives have been spared, how close we came to being at the intersection when the accident happened and we could have been involved. You will never know in your life, what infectious germs touched your body but never took root so you never became ill! Yes, thank

God for storms which blew out, blew over, passed you by, never touched you. God shows His goodness to you in many ways.

#5. Be thankful for friends, old and new.

When disappointments hit, stop and recall old friends. If you're down and discouraged, take time and write on a piece of paper the friends that have meant the most to you in your life. Go back to your childhood: Who was the little girl or the little boy you walked to school with? Who was your favorite teacher? Who was the favorite friend on your block? Who was the schoolmate? Think of all these friends, the old ones, the present ones, and the new ones, and then stop and think: "Some of the best friends in your life you haven't even met yet!" Surely the love of friends is like the hand of God reaching out to comfort you.

Today, tomorrow, this week, this year you are going to meet new people for the first time. I predict that some of the best friends you'll ever meet are still waiting to be met. Through them, you will experience the goodness of God.

#6. Be thankful for impossibilities that became possibilities.

It is easy to forget past blessings. We can get so blinded by something that isn't happening today that we focus on the unanswered prayers instead of the answered prayers. We look at what is denied us instead of what we have left. We get hung up on our failures instead of on our triumphs, our successes and our achievements. God says to us, "Be thankful always for all good things."

Think of the impossibilities that became possibilities. When I become discouraged, I come and stand in

this Cathedral and remember when this fantastic building was just one great big, wild, impossible idea! Engi-
neers told me, "You can't build a building out of glass
that big in an earthquake zone."

But we did it and it has survived some pretty good
shakes. Thank God for impossibilities that became possibilities.

#7. *Be thankful for gifts, given and received.*

Pause and think about the gifts you've received, but
most of all, thank God for the joy of giving. Early in our
ministry, my wife would urge me at times of discouragement to call on members of the church who were
shut in. I would visit them and give them an uplifting,
encouraging thought. In the process, I discovered a
really great truth: It is impossible to give of yourself
without receiving something immediately. "Do not fret
because of evil doers. Trust in the LORD, and do
good" (Ps. 37:1, 3).

Disappointed? Go out and prepare a gift, make
something. I recall my mother had her times of disappointment; those were tough years growing up in the
depression in Iowa. But she would pick apples from the
tree; she would peel them; she would make an apple
pie. It cost her only a few cents. She would bring it to
somebody in the community that either just had a baby
or lost a husband or was sick and in bed.

Thank God for gifts given and for gifts received.

#8. *Be thankful for possibilities that God put within you.*

There are possibilities within each of us that have
been discovered and developed. There are others that
remain undiscovered, undeveloped, and give me the
frontier edge of potential progress in the weeks and

months to come. So, be thankful for possibilities that are blossoming. Be thankful that the world hasn't seen the best of you yet. If you're not happy with what you see, stick around. God is still at work.

Consider the attitude reflected in this prayer by Cardinal Richard Cushing. Gene Autry, country-western star and owner of the California Angels, has carried it in his pocket since he heard Cardinal Cushing share it in 1973:

> "Dear God,
>
> Help me be a good sport in this game of life. I don't ask for an easy place in the line up. Just put me where you need me. I'll only ask that I can give you 100% of all I have. If the hard drives seem to come my way, I thank you for the compliment. Help me remember that you never send a player and have him do more than he can handle. Help me, Oh, Lord, to accept the bad breaks as part of the game. And may I always play the game on the square no matter what the others do. Help me study the books so that I can know the rules. Finally, God, if the natural turn of events go against me and I am benched for sickness or old age, please help me to accept that as part of the game, too. Keep me from whimpering or squealing that I was framed or that I ruined a deal. And when I finish the final inning I ask for no laurels. All I want is to believe that in my heart I played as well as I could. Amen"

#9. Be thankful for hope that springs eternal and never dies.

The Keenagers, the Sunday School class of Senior Citizens, planted a tree here at the Crystal Cathedral. If you visit this church, you will see a Norfolk pine tree. If you walk up to the Norfolk pine, you will see a granite plaque that reads, "A gift to the Crystal Cathedral Congregation in the year 2007, by the Keenagers Class of 1987."

Each year, the Keenagers buy another tree and plant it. In twenty years, the first tree will be sixty feet tall and then, each year, one will be cut down, lifted through the open doors and become the Christmas tree for the congregation.

Talking to the Keenagers, I said, "Do you know what it means to plant a tree? When you plant a tree, it means you have faith in tomorrow."

Redumption or Redemption?
Junk or Antiques?
It All Depends on How You View It!

My only brother, Henry, moved onto the original family farm site when he got married. My brother ran the farm much the same way Dad did, with one addition—The Dump. Henry dug out a huge pit where neighbors could come and dump their trash (for a small fee). Old couches, sagging mattresses, broken chairs, rusty toys, tins with costume jewelry, ragged coats, boots, you name it. JUNK—with a capital J.

Or was it? When my children visited Henry at the farm, their favorite place to play was—you guessed it— the dump. They dug through the trash with great delight. Some days they looked for copper items, aluminum odds and ends. They found an old copper wash tub, an aluminum tray. All of these items were loaded onto a wagon until the wagon could hold no more. The treasure was carefully pulled across the pasture, past the fields, around the barn, and unloaded on the back porch of the farm house.

"Look, Aunt Alberta! Look Uncle Henry! Look what we found!"

The copper tubs and aluminum items were taken to the metals plant and cashed in for a penny a pound and a nickel a pound. The children got nearly a dollar for a wagon-load of aluminum and copper antiques.

Alberta told the children later when they were grown up that she got the biggest charge out of the junk they would drag back from the dump to the farm house. She always pretended to admire their discoveries, but she admitted that she always brought everything back to the dump once the children had gone home to California.

Thirty years ago, those junk items were considered worthless by everybody but children. Today some of those items would fetch a good price in an antique store. Junk? Or priceless antique? It depends on how you view it and what you decide to do about it.

Alberta took the "junk" the children brought home and she re-DUMPED it all. She brought it back to the dump. Most of that trash belonged there.

The children weren't the only ones who loved to go to the dump. My father also scoured the pile of junk looking for things to fix and restore. His favorite find was an old toy. He would take home with him a box of broken toys. I loved to watch Dad work in the damp old basement where he had his workshop. His stack of old cigar boxes held oddly shaped nuts and bolts and screws. His gnarled hands, now shaky in his golden years, would pick up a bent, rusty, broken toy. He would patiently tap, sand, and reshape old metal sides. He would scour his boxes for a tire or two, and dab on a bright coat of shiny paint.

Before my eyes a raggedy old train tooted, a broken

dump truck dumped again, rusty gears began to grind again, new wheels started to roll, and bright colors spun like a rainbow. Old toys were like new, sometimes even better than new. They had been touched by a master and as they bumped and dumped and whirred, they reminded me of the power of redemption, versus reDUMPtion.

We have faced this choice in our lives at one time or another. To DUMP or to REDEEM? When your dreams come crashing down, you say, "Oh, Doctor Schuller. I don't have any choice but to dump my dream. There's nothing left. The doctors have told me it's useless. Why encourage me to go hitting my head against a brick wall?"

I hear your objections. I believe you when you tell me how hopeless your situation is. I can see why you are at the point where you are going to dump your dream. But before you do, listen to the story of Ana Maria Trenchi De Bottazzi. I first heard of Ana Maria when she wrote me a letter and told me her amazing story. After you have read her story, you may decide that you will want to give your dream ONE MORE TRY!

Ana Maria began piano studies at the age of two with her mother, the well-known Argentine pedagogue Ana Sieiro de Trenchi, and gave her first solo recital in her native Buenos Aires when she was four. As a child prodigy she toured many countries, and by the time she was eighteen, she had performed in solo recitals and with orchestras throughout South America, Europe, Africa, and Asia.

At the age of fourteen, she won a much-coveted French government scholarship for four years of study at the Conservatoire Nationale de Musique in Paris. There, at fifteen, she was awarded first prize for the best foreign student, and subsequently earned the prestigious Premiere Prix. After her first world tour when she was twenty-three years old, the French government sent her to Japan for two years as a full professor for graduate piano students at the Kunatachi University in Tokyo.

Then it happened. This gifted, world-renowned concert pianist was nearly killed in a serious automobile accident in Brussels. That was in 1962. The doctors were honest. The damage to certain parts of her brain were extensive. She would never play the piano again.

In 1990, Ana wrote me a letter. It was her first letter to me and through it I became familiar with one of the most remarkable women in music today. With her permission, I share parts of her letter.

> *To Dr. Schuller; my third maker.*
> *My first maker was God.*
> *My second maker was my mother.*
> *My third maker was Dr. Schuller,*
> *who helped me to*
> *become a full human being again.*

> *Dear Dr. Schuller:*
> *Today is my birthday and I don't have my mother or my father with me anymore. Therefore, I need to write to you: my third maker.*
> *I have "known" you for such a long time, and you have been such an influence in my life and career that I feel silly trying to introduce myself to you. I feel deep down that you also know me the way I know you.*
> *I am going, however, to tell you about two important things in my life: my accident and my coming to live in this country.*
> *Twenty-nine years ago, I had a horrible car accident in Brussels, and I almost died. I was hospitalized in Paris for five months, had ten hours of brain surgery and was*

*told that I would never play the piano again. For years to
come I couldn't do anything; remember anything. The doctors removed fifteen blood clots from the brain. I was paralyzed on the right side. I lost four of the five languages I
knew including my own language of Spanish. I only kept
the French for some reason.*

*I couldn't pick up a plate. I not only lost memory, I
lost coordination. I could not do what I wanted. It was
like something in my brain and my body was cut in between.*

*The doctors said, "Get married. Have children. Enjoy
life."*

*But I could not enjoy life if I didn't play the piano,
because my soul is my love of music. I need to play the
piano.*

*So, I went back again and again and would try to
move my first finger. The second finger moved instead. So
I had to retrain myself. This was long and painful. But I
kept it up.*

*My mother and my husband never believed the doctors.
       ⋯ould say to me over and over again, "What we
are ⋯ ⋯'s gift to us. What we become is our gift to God."
She told me over and over again that God doesn't make
mistakes. If He had given me a talent to play the piano,
He wanted me to use it.*

*For years and years I watched your program. I taped it
every Sunday and played it again and again during the
week. I have read each one of your books. Every time I had
a doubt, I would go to one of your books or tapes and I
would say, "I can do it! I can do it!"*

*I did that for sixteen years. And throughout the day I
would close my eyes. I would imagine myself playing at
Carnegie Hall. Then the people were giving me a standing
ovation. That was going to be my gift to God.*

*Sixteen years later I finally walked onto the stage at
Carnegie Hall. I was terrified. But I sat down and I*

prayed. I asked God to help me. I played for two hours. I was totally immersed in the music. I finished the last piece of music. I faced the audience. Two thousand people were clapping, giving me a standing ovation. For a second, I wasn't sure that it was really happening. It was exactly like my daydreams. When I realized it was real, I broke down and cried on the stage.

As I took my bow I said to myself, "God. This is my gift to you."

Sincerely,
Ana Maria de Bottazzi

That was just the beginning of her comeback. She has since given ten more concerts at Carnegie Hall. She has acquired her doctorate in piano from the Juilliard School of Music. Her husband, likewise, holds a doctorate in music. She continues to perform for government leaders and dignitaries throughout the world.

Not bad for a girl who was told she would never play again. Not bad for a young couple who came to America as penniless immigrants.

It would have been really easy for Ana Maria to have DUMPED her dream of playing the piano. No one would have blamed her. She had every right to quit. But her heart wouldn't let her. Her life's passion called her again and again to work at the impossible. She was broken in body and in bank account, but alive in spirit. So rather than choosing re-DUMPtion, she chose redemption. She called on God's help and revived, renewed, REDEEMED her dream. As a result she has given the gift of herself to God. She has given the gift of exquisite music to the world.

She's a believer—Life's not fair, but God is good!

CHAPTER SEVEN

Violated?
Victimized?
Mistreated?
DISCOVER FREEDOM
THROUGH FORGIVENESS

Who are the victims of life's injustices? They are people —probably just like you.

- Affirmations were unspoken.
- Recognition was neglected.
- Honors were withheld.
- Credit was deferred.
- Compensation was inadequate.
- Apologies were never offered.
- Forgiveness offered was spurned.
- Friendship was never returned in kind.

- Criticism was unjustified.
- Judgment was extreme—and unjust.

Life's really serious victims are the abused, violated human beings who have suffered real injury—profound loss and torturing pain. Life has been unfair to these people.

It is easy to find victims these days. Tragically, there are millions of wounded people walking the streets—and they're not all homeless. Some of them drive fancy cars. Some of them live in beautiful homes. Some of them carry important calling cards in their pockets. But if you were to find them in a vulnerable moment, you would hear the pain that walks with them every day.

Unresolved, untreated wounds that have been allowed to fester for years, eating at hearts, robbing lives of joy, can be detected in every community, at every economic strata. If you could develop an X-ray that could scan hearts and pinpoint emotional cancers, you would be amazed to see the epidemic that is spreading rampant through the world. Anger. Rage. Depression. Self-depreciation. The spectrum is wide. Who are the victims? Could YOU be one of these? Did you fail to get your fair share?

Victims of Neglect

All of us have felt the emotional pain of neglect at one time or another. It is real. You can find emotional neglect in any home. All parents are guilty of it from time to time. For some of us it is a matter of survival. The economics of our day are such that in many families one income is not enough. Two incomes are NECESSARY to SURVIVE. What does that mean to children?

It means that Mom is tired when she comes home from work to do more work—cooking, cleaning, and laundry. It means that Mom is wrung out and probably not able to be emotionally nourishing after waiting on tables, or balancing account sheets, and fighting the traffic. After a full day of work, she still has to pick up kids at day care, dump her work on a counter, kick off her heels, pull dinner out of the fridge, get the kids to bed or plop them in front of the television, while she does the dishes and the laundry. That's just for starters.

Is it fair to ask her to also provide emotional nourishment for her children? To read them poems, to listen to their questions, to play games, to tuck them in bed with a prayer? Is it fair to ask the children to go without?

It's easy to say, "Tomorrow." But tomorrows pile up until they're only a collection of lost "yesterdays."

It's not fair for Mom to be so tired that she can't enjoy her children. It's not fair for kids to be denied those intimate moments with Mom and Dad. The unfairness cuts both ways. But that's life for many families. That's a reality.

Speaking of emotional neglect—what about spouses? There is an awful lot of loneliness in marriage today. People die from starvation. Marriages die from loneliness. Couples grow apart. Selfish attitudes creep in. One spouse neglects the other. Sometimes it's subtle: "I'll get back at you. I won't talk to you anymore." Other times it's an escape. It's much easier to watch television or read the paper than to talk about things that matter, things that can nourish your partner's spirit.

We ALL need encouragement. We all need understanding. This is not a luxury. Whether we are parents, whether we are spouses, whether we are employers, positive emotional support systems are a necessary entity if we are going to live fulfilled lives.

A flower will wither and wilt and eventually die if it isn't watered. When was the last time you were watered? When was the last time you were nourished? When was the last time someone lavished undivided attention on YOU?

Do Your Share to Make Life Fair

Don't wait for the nourishment to come to you. If you are crossing the desert and have run out of water, you don't just lie down and wait for the rain to fall in your mouth. That's folly. Yet, that's what many of us do when it comes to emotional nourishment. We sit at home and mope about how lonely we are. "Nobody loves me." We sing the blues and drown in depression because life isn't fair. We forget God is good.

If you feel emotionally deprived, if you are starving for emotional nourishment, then do yourself a favor. Find a positive support group and get yourself plugged into an organization that will begin to nourish you. It may be a small group at a local church. It may be a community service group. It may mean calling old friends that you have neglected and being honest, "I'm sorry I've been so busy lately. I've missed you. Can we get together?"

Look for the oasis. If you search hard enough, it just may find you. And when you find it, drink long and hard of the refreshment. Rest and renew your soul. Make a commitment to visit the well frequently. Don't ever let yourself get that dehydrated again. There are too many people who need you. There are people who are suffering far worse than you have. Perhaps you have only faced neglect. As hurtful and potentially damaging as that is, neglect is corrected fairly easily. The damage caused by abuse can take a lifetime to repair.

We are ALL victims, but to say that we have all suffered to the same degree as someone else is not accurate, nor is it healthy. That is not to say that ALL pain isn't real. If you have first degree burns—that HURTS! If you have second degree burns—that hurts, too. But third degree burns are said to inflict the greatest pain that mankind can endure.

Who is to say that a little burn doesn't hurt? It does! The difference is not in the amount of pain as much as it is in the recovery process. A minor burn will heal quickly. It will probably heal on its own. A little cold water and after an hour or so, the burn is more than likely forgotten. You wouldn't go to the emergency room if you touched a hot kettle. You wouldn't fear gangrene or permanent scarring.

The same is true for those of us who have been victims of minor neglect. I have heard many of your tales of woe. I have heard that your parents neglected you or your spouse left you alone too many nights. As we've said, that hurts. Your pain is real. But your pain is like a burned finger. It's really not too serious. Don't overreact. Don't make it into something bigger and more painful than it really is, no matter how unfairly you have been treated.

This kind of pain is something that you can fix. You can make it better with a little bit of time and attention. You may have to take the bull by the horns; you may have to make the first move. But you can do it. And it will be worthwhile.

On the other hand, there are those of you who have suffered third degree burns. You have not only been neglected, you have been abused, battered, beaten in mind, spirit, and perhaps even in body. You need emergency treatment. Call the paramedics. Send up the flares. Take the ambulance to the emergency room. Don't think that your pain will go away by itself. You wouldn't try to treat a third degree burn by yourself. If you are a victim of abuse, don't try to treat your emotional pain by yourself. Get help—NOW!

VICTIMS OF ABUSE

I will never forget the day when I was standing in line at a men's store. I was waiting to be helped. A woman directly in front of me was making her purchase. Next to her stood a man, larger than she. While the clerk was ringing up her purchase, she looked at the young man and said, her voice dripping in sarcasm, "Looks like you got some sun today." Then she looked at the clerk and said, "He skipped school again today."

The clerk responded, "What college do you go to?"

"Not college, high school. That's his trouble. He's got the body of a man, but the brains of a baby."

At that point the young man turned around and walked fast out of the store. His mother was still signing the credit slip. Inside I cried for that young man. Nobody deserves to be treated like that.

Emotional abuse is not an occasional remark. It is not an oversight. *It is a day to day barrage of garbage!* It is an overwhelming imbalance of negative words over positive words. What that mother did to her son was ABUSE! And it was NOT FAIR.

There are children who are abused emotionally by their parents. There are spouses who are emotionally abused by their husbands or wives. Their words are negative, negative, negative. They inflict one wound upon another. There are other children who are abused physically. There are women who are victims of incest. There are boys who are sexually abused. There are women who are victims of rape, and women who are beaten by their boyfriends or husbands.

These victims are victims of ABUSE. Life has treated them unfairly. And their wounds are deep. They are life-threatening. They cannot be healed with a simple renewzit program. Those kinds of wounds take a LIFETIME of work and support. We have at the Crystal Cathedral a ministry that is comprised of specialized small groups. Some of those groups deal with victims. The groups are led by a beautiful Christian minister. She was trained and ordained and has since specialized in working with a ministry to women who are victims. Her name is Linda Bos. I went to Linda and asked her some questions regarding the trauma that victims face and how they can overcome it.

Linda's statistics were staggering. She said, "Dr. Schuller, did you know that one out of three women are sexually abused before eighteen years of age? One out of six men are abused before reaching adulthood. Spousal abuse (such as wife battering) occurs in thirty-three percent of all marriages."

I was astounded. Frankly I was doubtful. "Do you mean to tell me that one out of every three women who will read this book are victims of sexual abuse?" I asked.

"Most likely."

It was still hard to believe the magnitude of the problem. "And one out of every six men who buy this book will have been abused?" I countered.

"Yes."

I didn't want to believe what I was hearing, but as a pastor, I knew from experience that what Linda says is true. I gulped and asked her, "And thirty-three percent of the women who will be reading this section on victims will have experienced abuse first hand by their husbands?"

"Probably."

It took a moment for the implications of these numbers to sink in. I said to this colleague of mine, "Then this section of the book will be of prime importance. It will be touching lives that have felt the deepest and the most devastating hurts possible."

"I'm afraid that's true."

"You are the expert. These victims need to know that God is good. Help us walk through this difficult but necessary passage. Guide us, Linda. What's the first step?"

"Well, Dr. Schuller, the first step is admitting that you are a victim. Shame is a typical response to remembering the abuse (victims of incest often repress the incest until their mid-thirties or beyond). The victim is embarrassed to tell of her abuse—whether it is of childhood abuse or current abuse (as in rape). The victim feels like she is defective; that something is wrong with her."

"How tragic! The victim suppresses the abuse and thereby denies herself any help that she could have received."

"Yes."

"After a victim has admitted that he or she is a victim, then what's the process?"

"The process is lifetime work. There are common issues among those who have been victimized: low self-esteem, broken trust and the resulting poor choices in relationships, depression, anger, shame. It can take years of work to overcome just one act of abuse—rape, incest, physical abuse. The victim is left not knowing if she can trust other people or herself."

"If the process takes a lifetime," I asked her, "Is there hope for recovery to the point where the victim can lead a full and productive life again?"

"Oh, yes. The primary pivot point comes when the

victim can place the full blame for the abuse on the abuser and not on herself (or himself). It is essential to come to the belief that there is nothing a child can do that deserves abuse; there is absolutely nothing that a victim of rape has done that deserves to be raped. They have been dealt with unfairly. Dispelling these myths are essential to getting out of the endless trap of self-blame. Until the victim can begin to accept that she was *not responsible* for the abuse, she will have a difficult time healing. Feeling responsible for the abuse keeps her feeling lonely, isolated, and guilty."

I said, "So, the first step is admitting you are a victim."

"Yes."

"And the second step is placing the guilt on the abuser."

"Yes. *The guilt belongs to the abuser.* This is the most difficult concept for victims. They are filled with reasons why the abuser did what he/she did. Putting the responsibility where it belongs frequently means admitting that the family was wrong. These feelings hurt too much as the victim gives up the illusion of family harmony. Children will frequently find the badness within themselves rather than their parents, whom they long for and love. If abused children were to see their parents as bad, they would be jeopardizing their most important relationship. Since they see themselves as extensions of their parents, accepting parents as bad also inevitably means accepting themselves as bad."

As Linda talked, I was beginning to get a new sense of victims—who they are and what they face. I was beginning to appreciate the hard work they have to do if they want to get free from their hurts. I said, "Let me ask you one more question. The victim has admitted that she is a victim. How does she get to this pivotal point where she can place the responsibility where it belongs?"

"She can join a support system such as the groups we have in the Crystal Cathedral. There are groups in every community that are designed to help. She can read some helpful books on the subject. My favorites are *Outgrowing the Pain* by Eliana Gil, *Recovering From Rape* by Linda E. Ledray, and *Incest and Sexuality: A Guide to Understanding and Healing,* by Wendy Maltz and Beverly Holman."

She continued, "The fact is, Dr. Schuller, that this is an unjust world. Bad things do happen to good people. Freedom and healing occur when this is acknowledged and the pain of the event is able to be shared. Healing comes when the victim begins to doubt her own perceptions. She needs good support to clear up the distortions and to set the scene for reality.

"Part of the reality is to know that God has been with the victim the whole time—not allowing the abuse, but with the victim and has been hurt with her. God's history is being with those who are hurting. He wants to bring healing. In this broken world, people make terrible choices and hurt other people. God's grace is such that when we ask for forgiveness for those bad choices, then God is willing to forgive. It's crucial for the victim to know that her abuser can only be truly forgiven by God when she or he asks for that forgiveness."

We are all victims. We have all felt pain. Ironically, it is the person who has faced a minor pain who feels free to seek help. It is the ones who have been devastated by searing pain that are unable to admit that they need help. They hide in shame. They deny their pain. They protect their violator and suppress their rage.

Healing comes when we can admit that we are vic-

tims. Forgiveness starts when we can place full blame
on the violator.

ONLY VICTIMS CAN FORGIVE

Someone has hurt you. You can't forgive until you
have admitted that you have been hurt. It's O.K. to feel
angry. In fact that is a much healthier stance than de-
nying the pain and hiding in shame. Admit your pain.
Seek help. And then remember—YOU CAN DO IT!
You can get better. You can heal. You don't have to be
a victim any more. You can walk away from a destructive situation and begin to build your life again. Don't
take my word for it. Take Francine's:

Dear Dr. Schuller,

*Ten years ago, I ran away from a wife-abuse situation
with two children, one turtle, one dog, and four pieces of
clothing packed in one suitcase. We took the automobile
which was nearly eight years old, leaving the new Cadillac
for my abusing spouse, a dignified business man whom I
married in 1956. I sought help from the priests, but they
weren't trained at that time to understand abuse.*

*In the meantime, I tried to placate my husband by
being the perfect wife. Nothing helped. What my children
have gone through is indescribable. Horror pervaded their
young lives, behind closed doors, in an affluent neighborhood.*

*I took it for twenty-one years. But when my children
were nearing their teens, I suddenly got the courage to seek
help. The help I found was through two lawyers. A husband and wife team, they dried my tears, picked me up
and said, "You can do it, Francine."*

*It meant providing a living for myself as well as my
two children. I had always wanted to finish college, so I
looked for a job at the University of Pittsburgh. I was hired*

by the university and began to build my new life. I plunged into my new responsibilities as a provider for my two children, AND I went back to school.

I want you to know, Dr. Schuller, that I not only survived—I grew! On April 28, 1990, I received my Ph.D. I met a widower who has become my new husband. We were married by two priests who knew my life-long struggle to find a relationship with dignity, a nonviolent home, and the freedom to grow as an individual without oppression.

I am glad to be alive to live for Jesus. He strengthens me and reminds me to trust. "For He has appointed a time for every matter, and for every work." Ecclesiastes 3:17

Respectfully submitted,

Dr. Francine Dennis-McCauley

THE VIOLATORS—WHO ARE THEY?

The violators aren't just gang members. They're not just drug addicts. They're men and women like you and me. They are parents, teachers, preachers, doctors, lawyers—any one who is in a position of control or domination. Anyone who uses their power to hurt instead of heal is a violator. Don't think that this problem exists only in derelict societies. It happens in more affluent homes than you would care to think.

Men who batter have become a national concern. Emergency shelters exist across the country for women and their children to escape these madmen who cannot control their rage. We have spent a great deal of time and money providing these necessary places of refuge.

My daughter and her husband tell of the time they were shopping in a luxurious mall here in southern California. In the middle of one of the richest stores a beautiful girl, about eight years old, walked next to a man. The girl had cascades of long, blonde curls. She was crying. Her hand was held over her heart. The man gripped her arm as he led her out of the store. His icy eyes carefully avoiding contact with the other shoppers who were beginning to turn and stare. Through the sobs my daughter could make out the words, "Please don't hit me!"

Now, all of us have seen children dragged from a store crying. Parents sometimes lose patience trying to shop with the little wiggle-worm. This was different. A chill ran through my daughter. Her husband looked at her with alarm. "We have to help her," he said.

They called security. By this time a small crowd had gathered. Other groups of people had also called for help. The same feeling of concern had been shared by others who had witnessed this man and the girl in his power. Security got the license plate number of the man's car. A social worker would be sent to the home to investigate. Then the security officer said, "This is not uncommon. We get calls like this all the time. Frequently it is child abuse." Oh, the unfairness in such treatment.

My daughter looked at her husband with tears in her eyes. They held hands, closed their eyes and prayed in that luxurious store for the nameless little girl, prayed to God that His goodness might protect the child.

THE MATTRESS AT THE BOTTOM OF THE CLIFF

There's no question that shelters are necessary. However, they are the mattress at the bottom of the cliff. We need to go to the top, to the people who are pushing their victims off the edge. Then we will be saving lives, not just repairing lives.

That means we have to help the violators. We have to be willing to create programs that will heal them, not just punish them. It is hard to help the violators. We are frequently so angry at them that we want to lock them up and put them away forever. The last thing we want to do is help THEM! We want to help the victims—and we should. And we will when we help the violators and remember that the violators were once victims too.

Donna Stone Pesche, daughter of W. Clement Stone, understood this. She devoted her inherited income and influence to become the first person to focus nationwide attention on the problem of child abuse. The motivation? Her mother had been abused as a girl. Donna gave generously of her time, her talents, and her finances to her cause before she died at too young an age of cancer. She left behind a flourishing awareness of child abuse that is saving lives today. "Parents who abuse their children are not monsters," she said. "They need help in dealing with their anger. They need to learn parenting skills."

We not only have support groups for the victims in our church, we also have a men's group for those who are unable to control their anger. The group is called Men at Peace. The Family Life pastor at the Crystal Cathedral, Dick Klaver, is also a therapist whose specialty is family systems and men's emotions. He has developed a program that has had tremendous success at our church and has written a book on the subject of men and their emotions.

He is attempting to deal with the man at the top— the man who is unable to control his anger and who is pushing women and children over the edge of the cliff. Now, most people shudder when they think of working with these men. It is hard to be sympathetic. It is hard to be understanding. But that is just what these men need. They need someone who can help them identify the root source for their anger. Dick calls it the *angst*— the root hurt that manifests itself as either anxiety or anger. He points out that the root word for both anxiety and anger is *angst*. Then he helps men work on healing that sore spot.

One of the first steps in dealing with these men is to address the issue of substance abuse. Drugs and alcohol mixed with out of control emotions is a dangerous combination. The first step is dealing with the substance abuse—joining A.A. or another twelve-step program. Such a program, combined with a helpful support group that deals specifically with healing a hurt, is prescribed for many men who hurt.

Violators can be turned into victors with the right kind of support, with the right kind of treatment and with the right kind of people who believe in them. It is possible for violators to be redeemed when they run smack into the healing, redeeming power of love.

John Morel was the mayor of Darlington, England. One day, while walking to his office, he saw a member of his town. This man had once been a leading citizen who had been convicted of crime and sentenced to three years in jail. Now he was out for the first time. The mayor said, "Hello, I'm glad to see you."

The man didn't answer. He just turned and, embarrassed, walked off fast. Years later, that man had built a successful business, created job opportunities, became a contributor and a generous builder of the church. He was beloved in the whole community and was honored by his city. At his awards banquet the man approached the mayor. He said, "Mayor Morel, I want to thank you for all you've done for me."

The mayor looked at him with surprise. Puzzled, he said, "What do you mean? I've done nothing for you.

You've never been in my office. We've never spoken before."

The man said, "Oh, but you have. You spoke to me the day I came out of jail. I met you. You said hello to me. You spoke a kind word to me and it changed my life."

THE VICTORS—WHO IS ABLE TO OVERCOME THE HURT?

Is it possible to be a victor? Is it possible to forgive? Is it possible to make roses out of ashes?

Yes. Yes. Yes. It's not easy. Forgiving is probably the hardest task we may face in our lifetimes. Yet the alternative is unthinkable—life filled with bitterness, hate, anger. There is nothing sweet about revenge. It may help to remind yourself that only to the victim of unfairness, injustice, or abuse is given the glorious opportunity to offer pardon and forgiveness!

The foundation of my faith—of Christianity—is forgiveness. The tap root of my belief system is mercy. We Christians believe in wiping the slate clean. We believe in new chances. Repairing the breaches. We follow a Leader who lived and died for forgiveness.

When Peter asked Jesus, "Lord, how often shall my brother sin against me, and I forgive him? . . . seven times?" Jesus said to him, "I do not say to you, up to seven times, but up to seventy times seven" (Matt. 18:21–22).

Yet forgiveness has been difficult for me. I am human and like you I have had my share of hurts, pot shots, lies, betrayal hurled in my direction. I would be lying if I said all that didn't hurt. I have had to forgive and it has not always been easy. As a pastor I have learned as much in this area as I have taught. My people have taught me a lot about forgiveness. Through

FORGIVENESS
Is Where We Encounter . . .
GOD'S GOODNESS . . .

FACE
to
FACE . . .
HEART
to
HEART!

the years I have seen, time and again, powerful examples of true forgiveness. Let me give you just a few glimpses of some of the people who stand out in my memory as true VICTORS, no matter how unfairly life treated them.

The Rose Lady

The whole world knows that South Central Los Angeles has become a center of fear and violence. It is also the home of The Rose Lady.

Her real name is Esther DeBar. She and her husband moved into a home in South Central Los Angeles fifty years ago when they first got married. They saved up five hundred dollars for the down payment and bought their dream home. Her husband worked in Los Angeles, and they bought a home five miles from City Hall.

When they first moved into their charming little home, the community was really neighborly. They shared pumpkin pies with each other, borrowed cups of sugar, were involved in the PTA, worked in Boy Scouts. Then in the late fifties things began to change. The neighbors began to move out—to the beach or to the mountains. When they moved, the ethnic people from different parts of the world began to move in. Through the years, Esther's neighbors included people from Vietnam, Korea, the Philippines, Mexico. By 1960 all of the original neighbors were gone.

Esther and her husband decided to stay. Once upon a time they had wanted to be missionaries. As their neighborhood changed, they thought to themselves, *Why shouldn't we stay in our neighborhood and minister to our neighbors?* After all, they now had the whole world at their doorstep. They wanted to see the world, so this was a way to see it without going to any expense!

The house in which the DeBars lived was built in 1909. Consequently, it had an old building in the back of the yard that had originally been a stable for horses. That old building stood in the only sunny spot in her shaded back yard. Esther said that she often secretly wished that the old building wasn't there so she would have a sunny spot to plant roses. Then one night her next-door neighbors knocked on her door. They said, "A building in your back yard is burning!"

Esther ran out into the yard in her nightgown and watched her old building, her avocado tree, and all the other trees in her yard go up in flames. The firemen trampled all over her yard, working feverishly. Esther helped out with the garden hose. By three in the morning, the fire was out. The firemen had all left. The building was gone. Trees were gone. Furniture that had been stored in the building was gone—all was gone except one little chair. Esther sat down in that chair and surveyed the ghostly pile of ashes, glowing in the moonlight. She said to herself and to the Lord, "When the ashes cool, I'm going to plant a rose garden."

Three feet of ashes covered stone-hard dirt that had not been turned in nearly a century. Esther says that as she dug through the hard-as-rock dirt, she said to herself, "It's just like that preacher says on TV, *'Inch by inch anything's a cinch.'* "

Part of the beauty of roses is the way you plant them. They have to have a big hole for their deep roots. She started with thirty rose plants. Today, there are fifty in her yard. Then she started planting rose bushes on the grounds of her church. Those roses are distributed throughout South Central Los Angeles. If someone throws an empty pop bottle in her yard, she puts a beautiful rose in it and sets it on a neighbor's porch step. In the past ten years, hundreds of roses have been delivered by this lady now known throughout the area as "The Rose Lady."

A victim? Of gang violence? Of drugs? Of urban warfare? Esther encourages us to turn our ashes into rose gardens, to bloom where we are planted. She gives us the courage to be victorious—not victims.

Sonja Foster

I will never forget Sonja. This lovely young violinist knows what it is to be a victim. She also knows what it is to be a victor. Not once, but three times!

A talented musician, she attended Curtis Institute and Juilliard School of Music. These prestigious academies accept only the most promising musicians. Sonja was followed by a younger brother, Lawrence, who was likewise a talented musician. He was a gifted cellist, a true child prodigy. He soloed with the Philadelphia Orchestra, Chicago Symphony and many other famous orchestras from the time he was ten or eleven years old. Leonard Bernstein chose him to solo on the Young People's concerts on nationwide television.

Mr. Bernstein said about him, "Lawrence Foster is an authentic genius."

Sonja and her brother teamed up and performed concerts across the country. These two bright young musicians were close. They had been raised in a Christian home. Mom and Dad had brought both of them to church since the day they were born. That solid foundation bore Sonja up when she learned the tragic news that her brother had been brutally murdered at the age of twenty-six, by a car thief in Atlanta, Georgia.

I asked Sonja, "How did you get through such a horrible ordeal?"

She looked at me, straight-backed. Clear-eyed. "When you are faced with death, truly the only person that can get you through is God. I trusted the Lord. It was very, very difficult. I chose to follow through with the concerts that Lawrence and I had been scheduled to perform. I did the tour alone that we had been scheduled to give together."

"So God gave you the victory over the death of your beloved brother."

"Yes. Through the grace of God I was able to carry on, even though I missed Lawrence terribly. Three months after Lawrence was killed, I discovered that I was pregnant. Naturally my husband and I were delighted. It helped take the edge off the loss of my brother. I was looking forward to a new little life. However, in the sixth month of my pregnancy I developed eclampsia which is the leading killer of pregnant women. I had a seizure that killed my unborn child.

"I spent forty-five days in the hospital in Chicago, suffering through many life-threatening conditions. Among them was a blood clot in my heart and a clot on my liver. Many people were praying for me, so I feel that I am alive due to a miracle."

"Those were two big losses for any woman to endure—first your brother, then your unborn child."

"Yes. I was still reeling from those two blows when my marriage fell apart. The divorce was a terrible amputation. A horrible pain. But again, God was my strength. He does gird us with strength. I had listened to you, Dr. Schuller, for years on television and I had read every one of your books. God has used you in a mighty way in my life. Through you, God has given me beauty for ashes. You said, *God will have the last word, and it will be good.* I believed you. I wrote those words down and put them in my violin case. I read those words every time I took my violin out to practice."

"You believed me?"

"Oh, yes. And I'm glad I did, for those words gave

me hope. They carried me through the tough times. God has answered my prayers. I believe in the Lord with all my heart. He is my strength and my shield. He's given me a wonderful new husband as well as many new opportunities to perform around the country.''

What does this say? I translate this testimony to read: Life's not fair—but God is good.

Laura Cate

Laura Cate and her husband, Frank, are two of the stalwart pillars of the Crystal Cathedral. They are very active in the small groups and in the adult Bible class.

My wife and I were immediately impressed with both Laura and Frank, and when they invited us to dinner, we readily agreed. As I listened to her tales of working abroad in Vietnam, Germany, and Turkey as a club director for military recreation centers, I said, "Laura, you're a remarkable person. You had to have a remarkable father and mother. Tell me about them."

The sad story then came out. "Yes, my parents were very special. My mother was a person who was very capable of loving and giving. She was a strong person, spiritually and emotionally. She was a deeply religious person. She read the Bible and prayed and attended Mass daily. She often had to walk with a cane because she had severe arthritic feet and knee problems. But she walked and swam regularly. My father is an extrovert and very well liked by all, including his five sons who work with him in the general contracting business.

"My parents wanted us to be independent, but responsible for our own actions. They often emphasized that getting along in the family was more important than getting your own way. And I think today we have a very keen sense of family loyalty as the result."

My wife said, "You are very lucky to have such a close family."

Laura nodded. Her eyes filled. She said, "Dr. Schuller, I remember that you once said just a few seconds can change everything. It was that way with my family in November of 1982. On a Sunday afternoon, my parents were leaving a park in Shady Cove, Oregon, and were robbed at gunpoint. They gave the robber their money. Then the young man, with gun raised, insisted that they go into the woods because he said he wanted to tie them up. At this point they became afraid. There was no rope and it was obvious that this man was not going to take their money and simply run.

"My mother just flatly refused to go, so this man grabbed her and threw her down on the ground. My sixty-eight year old father jumped him but was shot three times. He fell to the ground. My mother who walked with her cane made a feeble attempt to defend herself. Obviously she was no match for this young man. She received multiple stab wounds and died right on the scene. The attacker then proceeded to stab my father."

I had to shudder. No one likes to hear such gruesome tales. My mind always spins at the thought of such cruelty. I can't comprehend how one human being can murder another. In spite of years of studying the human mind and spirit, I still cringe when I hear of such horror. I struggled to concentrate once again on Laura. She was saying, "All of this was going on while two lanes of traffic were whizzing by just a few yards away. Fortunately, someone finally noticed what was going on and came to Dad's aid; otherwise, we would have lost him as well."

My wife, Arvella, asked, "Then they caught the attacker?"

"Yes." Laura replied. Her voice was calm. No malice. No bitterness. "It took only a day to find him. He was eventually convicted and he's in jail today."

I looked with admiration at Laura. How could she tell us all this with such composure? I probed, as we pastors frequently do, for the emotions that I suspected were there—somewhere. "How do you feel toward this man?" I asked her, "I mean, it would be perfectly natural for you to be bitter, angry, hateful."

Laura took a deep breath. She said candidly, "The pain I felt at first was so intense that I really feared I would snap in two. I think that it's natural and healthy to grieve intensely, but at some point, the healing process has to begin. We have to let go of some of the anger."

I could tell that Laura had found her peace. I said, "Tell me, what was the turning point?"

"I had always had religious education growing up, but had not fully understood Jesus' promise of salvation. Nor had I made a personal commitment to Him. My mother died a terrifying death. But seconds before she died, something wonderful happened to her. I know this because she died with a smile on her face. Her smile really startled me later when I saw her in the funeral home. I've never forgotten that smile."

Laura smiled. She added, "I miss my mother very much. But I don't stand at her grave and weep. My father really paved the way for healing for all of us. We knew the young man and his family. It was, after all, a small town. Father quickly set the mood. He said that he was brokenhearted over losing his wife, but he reminded us that there was nothing we could do to bring mother back. We should believe that she was where she always wanted to be—in heaven. I followed my father's example. And I have accepted Christ's promise of eternal life as true for one reason—I know that Christ's promise is far better than anyone else's. And only recently I wrote the murderer a Christmas letter. I told him, *'I forgive you—as Christ forgave those who crucified Him.'* "

Bob Trueblood

Bob and Pam were devoted members of the Crystal Cathedral. They were active in a young family Sunday school class and were well-loved by their class members. Like all young families, their schedules were filled with school and extracurricular events, such as baseball, soccer, gymnastics. Their marriage was happy. Their home was a gathering place for neighborhood children. It was a fun place to be. A great place to live.

Bob celebrated Pam's thirty-sixth birthday on October 22 of 1984. They went out to dinner. The next morning, he kissed her good-bye, gave his kids a hug, and left for work. That was the last time he ever saw them alive. He worked late that afternoon. When he walked into the dark house, he heard the phone ringing. It was the mother of one of his son's friends. She was wondering where her son was. Pam had gone to pick up her own children and her neighbor's son from a gymnastics class two miles from the house. Usually Pam had dropped her boy off long before now.

Something was obviously wrong. There could have been car trouble. An accident. Bob went to look for them. He was stopped at a police barricade only blocks from the house. The policeman told him the grim news. His wife's car had been hit head-on by a drunk driver. Pam, Eric, and Kerry had all died at the scene. Scotty, the youngest, eight years old, had been rushed to the hospital. By the time Bob got there, Scotty had also died.

Bob spent the night at his brother's where, he said, "I cried all night. It undoubtedly was the toughest time in my life. Hopefully it will be the toughest thing I ever have to live through. That week was unbelievably horrible."

I was in Israel when I learned of the accident. I called Bob. We talked and he had the most unusual request. He told me how he and Pam had spent time in Jerusalem two years before. He said, "Dr. Schuller, would you go to the Garden Tomb (where tradition says Jesus was buried) and say a prayer for my family? That place meant a lot to me and Pam and it would help me to remember her as she was the day we visited that garden. It would help remind me that her life isn't really over, that there is new life for her and for my kids."

Naturally it was a moving time of prayer for me. I wept for this father and husband, now alone.

The funeral was overwhelming—four coffins—four hearses. Bob said, "The only thing that got me through the burial service was the fact that I realized that two thousand years ago, our heavenly Father, sent His Son, Jesus Christ, to die voluntarily for me and for the four I had just lost. I knew that my family was with their heavenly Father, and with Jesus. I didn't have to worry about them. I knew I had to worry about me. I had to worry about the other people who loved them.

"Tragedy has a way of changing you. And it's going to leave its mark on you. There's just no way you can go through an experience like that and not be changed. One of the first things you have to deal with is the responsibility of this thing. Whose responsibility was it? Was God at fault? Of course not! Was He punishing me for some terrible sin I had committed? No way! I rejected that thought because I know my heavenly Father still loves me. I know it's the sin of a drunken driver that caused that accident.

"I believe that we have two choices. Either we can

shake our fist at God, and blame Him for the accident, for the terrible tragedy, for all the loss. That leads to bitterness. That does nothing to fill the emptiness inside. Or, we can fall into His arms and seek refuge there and let Him strengthen us. I chose the latter.

"It's amazing all the people that He used to allow me to survive. I really didn't want to survive. I would come home from work and there would be forty or more letters from people across the country. I spent my evenings reading those letters. That was an unbelievable, tremendous help during the week. But weekends were a vast expanse of time and loneliness."

"We happened to be going into the holiday season. As you know, I had been a member of this church for about twelve years, and an active member of one of the adult Sunday school classes. The people in that class knew Pam; they loved her. And they supported me. The Sunday school class put on a cookie bake one weekend to bake cookies to give to the prison ministries. The weekends were so miserable that I decided to go. At that cookie bake I met a young lady, recently widowed, who had just moved out here from Ohio. We hit it off pretty well. I had figured that getting over the loss of my family, my wife, was something that was going to take years. But the Lord does things in miraculous ways. The Lord was merciful. I met Diane. Six months after the accident, we were married."

Today Bob has a new family. Diane had a beautiful daughter, from her first marriage, Anjanette, and today Bob and Diane have two healthy young sons from their marriage.

How do I translate this testimony?

Life's not fair—but God is good!

Forgiveness. It's impossible—on your own. All of these church members are linked together with their grief and their ability to forgive. Their secret? They all believe in Someone who has broken the bounds of life and death. They believe in the Prince of Peace, the author of new life, rebirth, forgiveness, and mercy. They all believe in Jesus Christ.

Christianity is a religion based on mercy. It is rooted in forgiveness. Of all the religions in the world, Christianity is the only belief system that accepts grace as its source of salvation. Every other religion is based on good works—work hard enough or be good enough and you will earn your salvation, your heaven, your Nirvana.

Christianity alone says, "You can't do it. No one is perfect. We all make mistakes. We all suffer from guilt and shame. We are all victims. But Jesus has died on the cross with these final words: "Father, forgive them, for they do not know what they do" (Luke 23:34). He has risen again. He has paid for my crime. He has paid for yours. The gift of salvation is FREE—no strings attached."

Accept God's Forgiveness or You'll Treat Yourself Unfairly!

For many of us, our battles aren't with others—they're with ourselves. We have been the one who has done the hurting. We struggle with shame, remorse, guilt. We all have done things that we wish we could undo. We have all said things that we knew were vicious and cruel. Most of us aren't guilty of stabbing, or shooting, or maiming, but most of us have wounded with our words or our omissions.

Life's not fair, BUT GOD IS GOOD. Forgiveness is where we run face to face with God's goodness. We can live with many things, but we cannot live in guilt and shame, we cannot live without experiencing God's forgiveness.

The Bible says, "As far as the east is from the west, So far has He removed our transgressions from us" (Ps. 103:12).

Look at the globe. Our understanding of geography tells us that if we run our finger along the equator we will keep going East, East, East. We never hit West, unless we suddenly change directions, pivot our finger and go the opposite direction. But take your finger and go from the North Pole to the South Pole. From North to South there is an equator—a definite beginning and ending place, but going East to West is like an unbroken circle; there is no beginning and no ending. This Bible verse, "As far as the East is from the West . . ." was written thousands of years ago, back in the days when the common view of the world was flat.

The author of this verse did not have the knowledge of geography that we do, unless of course, the author was inspired by the Creator, Himself. I believe that the Scriptures are God's Book to us. The Creator tells us that He has removed our transgressions from East to West, not from North to South. That implies that He has removed our sins forever from us. What a comfort that is. What a relief!

God has forgiven. That is a fact of life too. The gift is extended. God stands before you with a lovely gift. It is large, beautifully wrapped. He smiles at you and says, "For you. From me, with love."

Why are we so hesitant to accept the gift? We long for the gift of grace. Yet we are reluctant to reach out and receive it, unwrap it and grasp it to our bosoms. Why would we be so hesitant to accept so precious a gift?

Simple—we feel we don't deserve it.

That's exactly why we need it! We don't deserve it. That's why God's forgiveness is grace. And grace is God's love in action for people who don't deserve it. It is ours to take. Forgiveness is more than a gift—it is life. We are lost without it.

Take one case in point about a man I first heard through the letter he sent me in 1982. Now, he has published his story under the title R for Addiction. His name is Dr. W. Robert Gearing. He was a medical doctor. Surprisingly his life was messed up, shot full of drugs, narcotics, addictions, and alcohol. Then he tried to kill himself. He scrubbed up, pretending to be preparing for surgery, but instead he injected his veins with a drug that he thought would end his misery for good.

However, he regained consciousness. One of the prominent staff physicians was at his side.

Dr. Gearing had no doubt that he would be evicted from his position at the hospital.

Imagine his shock when the doctor said to him, "Bob, I have no intention of having you dismissed from the hospital. I've come to try and save you. All I want is for you to come to church with me."

Robert Gearing had tried everything else. He decided to try church as well. To his amazement, he found what he had been looking for. He encountered Jesus Christ and was spiritually born again.

This very day there are people who will experience the beginning of a change in their attitude. This change will be the beginning of salvation. "You shall call His name JESUS," the angel said, "for He will save His people from their sins" (Matt. 1:21). Salvation: from sin to glory, from addictions to freedom, from hell to heaven.

When we find salvation, then the shame is gone. We are saved from shame to self-esteem, dignity, a sense of glory. Only an act of divine grace can accomplish something so phenomenal as seen in the case of Robert Gearing.

There is also Jerry's story. I can still see the man

walking across the fields, east of my church. I did not know that he was escaping from the county jail a half a mile east of this property. As a prisoner he had seen the cross on the top of our Tower of Hope. His name was Jerry. He was desperate and knew he wasn't getting the help he needed in jail.

So, he broke out of jail with one purpose, to try to find religion! To try to find Jesus. He told us, "I just walked out of the jail."

Of course we talked to him, told him we cared, but explained that we had to notify the jail of his escape. When the authorities found out where Jerry had gone and why, they asked us if we'd like to take him under our wing.

So Jerry joined our church family. We grew to know him and love him. His life was messed up. He had been a worldwide sailor, and had worked as an engineer on many vessels. Then, in our church, he learned about the GREAT FORGIVER, Jesus Christ.

One day he said to me, "Dr. Schuller, I don't want you to come into the mechanical room of the church for the next six months."

He said, "You can go to your office, you can go to the church, but you cannot come in my mechanical room."

I was puzzled, but I agreed to his unusual request.

About seven months later he came bursting into my office in the Tower. He said, "Dr. Schuller, you can come to the mechanical room now."

So I followed Jerry to his "office," the mechanical room which is filled with air conditioning equipment, pipes, faucets, wheels and long bolts with nuts. I came into that room and I couldn't believe what I saw. Jerry had painted every square inch of that room. First he started with the ceiling. He painted it blue with silver stars. Then he painted the duct work red, purple, and pink. Every piece of iron in that room was painted.

I was overwhelmed. It was beautiful, especially when he explained why he had done it. He said, "This rainbow room is the way I feel inside now."

Now—doesn't that prove that life's not fair, but God is good?

CHAPTER EIGHT

Now—Be Fair to Yourself—BELIEVE!

"*And we know that* all things work together for good to those who love God, to those who are the called according to His purpose" (Rom. 8:28).

"We are more than conquerors through Him who loved us" (Rom. 8:37).

"If God is for us, who can be against us?" (Rom. 8:31).

Life's not fair! So now what?

#1 STOP! THINK BEFORE YOU ACT!

When life's not fair, the first thing to remember is to be careful. Be careful how you react and what happens to you. Learn from the wonderful people you've met in this book. When you cannot control what happens to you in life's unfairness—at least treat yourself fairly! Be fair to yourself. Choose to react positively—not negatively.

Think. Use your head. Life's not fair. But is God good? Absolutely! The proof is He has given you an intelligent brain. Use it. Think.

I remember sitting next to a man on a plane. I said to him, "What do you do?"

He responded, "I'm a pilot and I'm heading home."

"Oh," I nodded.

He continued, "I've been a pilot for twenty-five years."

I asked, "How did you get into it?"

He replied, "During the Second World War."

I was curious, "Did you ever have any close calls?"

"Yep," he answered and looked out the window as he illustrated, "The most dangerous flight I had was when I was on a bombing run over Tokyo Bay. I was heading down, preparing to drop a bomb load, when I got hit." He continued, "What saved my life was my training. In school we were taught that *when you get hit and you face a horrendous crisis—don't do anything—just think.*" He nodded and thought hard, as he added, "The hardest job was to not push a control. Intuitively —instinctively I wanted to do just that but I didn't touch a thing; I kept cool. And you know what?"

I looked at him. He had my undivided attention. He said, "If I had touched a button, I'd have been dead today. As it happened, I had already adjusted my controls to start the leveling off, putting me into the take-up process. Everything worked out fine."

When you face a crisis, the first thing to remember is to stop! Don't act. Just think.

#2—Ask Smart Questions

Life's not fair—why is it that way? "Why do bad things happen to good people?" is a question often raised. My answer? That's the wrong question. It's wrong because no one knows the answer. "Why" is the question God never will answer. When we ask "Why" we don't want an explanation—we want an argument. We want to argue—we don't want to accept. Life's unfair—that's a given—not a debate.

Likewise, God never answers the questions that begin with "When?" Such as, "When will this injustice cease? When will I be treated fairly?" Again and again in the Old Testament the people of God, in their suffering, cried out, "How long, oh Lord? Before You deliver us?" And never—never did God answer.

Ask smart questions, like, "What" will I do about this? Like: "What" are my options? Like: "What" do I have left? Like: "How" shall I respond? Will my reaction to what's happened make matters better or worse? Will it attract strong and good support? Can I turn this obstacle into an opportunity? Is there some good that could possibly come out of this bad scene? Is this a final defeat—or a temporary setback? Am I "finished"? If so, I'll choose the final finish—with a glow!

#3—Be Slow in Passing Negative Judgment

That injustice, that lost job, that business failure, that financial loss, that unfaithful friend—be slow to condemn. Be wise and reserve judgment. This, too, may turn out to be a blessing in disguise.

Is the grinding wheel that puts a fresh edge on the knife, or the hoe that breaks up hard soil and plows out weeds, or the sharp knife or the gardener that prunes and snips useless growth to give greater strength to the roots and the trunk, or the north wind that forces the pine to send down roots of steel into granite earth, or the rod in the shepherd's hand that strikes the sheep lest it run blindly off a precipice, or the bloody surgeon's scalpel that cuts away the foreign tumor, or the sculptor's hard hammer and brutal chisel that chip and polish—are these not all our friends? The chisel, the hammer, the scalpel, the rod, the wind, the knife, the hoe, the wheel, are these not our friends?

Trouble is not always trouble! It is often God's way of making us lie down, turn around, sit still, pray, work harder, or start over again!

When is trouble not trouble, you ask? When it protects you from an unknown hazard on the road ahead, or shelters you from a sin that, unknown to you, lurks furtively in your path waiting to tempt and trip you, then trouble is not trouble!

When trouble cleans up cluttered clutter that you valued too highly and did not have the courage to discard or destroy, or when it tears out of your life an unworthy friend whom you were unable to help and who was not a good influence on your life, then trouble is not trouble!

When trouble makes you furious enough to fight for a good cause you were too busy to serve, or frustrates you so that you quit a job that was too long hiding your real talents and forces you to discover new skills and hidden talents that were lying undetected like veins of gold under cabbage fields, then trouble is not trouble!

When trouble causes two parties, long unspeaking, to bury the hatchet; when it makes a person forget himself and start thinking of others; when it makes a greedy man generous, a hard man compassionate; a cold heart warm, a thoughtless man considerate—then trouble is not without its reward!

When trouble teaches you valuable lessons that you would have been too blind to see, too arrogant to believe, or too stubborn to accept any other way than by this bed of pain; when it slams a door in your face to force you out of a rut that you would never have had the courage to leave and leads you down a new road through an open door, then trouble may be a most valuable experience!

When trouble stirs up gratitude for gifts you have taken too long for granted, or creates an opportunity for you to think, read, write, pray, then trouble is really a friend who comes to your door wearing your enemy's jacket!

So often trouble is only a part of the painful growing process like a seed buried alive by a seemingly merciless fate under suffocating ground in a windowless grave, until in supreme agony it ruptures into a new life! This death, burial, pain, is not trouble! It is the travail of new birth! "Unless a grain of wheat fall into the ground and dies, it remains alone; but if it dies, it produces much grain" (John 12:24).

When trouble breaks your heart and makes your knees buckle, and forces penitent tears from eyes sealed in prayer to Almighty God, then trouble may turn out to be the redeeming agony before new birth!

Just what kind of people do you think we would be if we never had any trouble! For we build hard muscles in heart and body when we lift heavy loads. Tough times makes callouses that may some day save our hands from bleeding! How right is Holy Writ, "But he who loves him disciplines him promptly" (Prov. 13:24).

Truly, we learn courage when we face danger; we learn patience when we endure suffering; we learn tenderness when we taste pain; we learn to prize true friends when false ones forsake us; we treasure health when illness strikes and we learn to prize freedom when we are in danger of losing it! Without trouble we would be like plants that have sprouted, grown, and been nurtured in the overprotected shelter of a hothouse, too tender ever to live in the open!

We have matured as Christians when we learn that there is no progress without pain; there is no conversion without crises; there is no birth without painful travail; there is no salvation without agonizing repentance and no Easter without a Good Friday! There is no service without suffering. What good would an ox be if it refused to wear a yoke?

So you are having trouble? You feel cheated and abandoned by God? Remember: The eagle stirs up the nest in order that the young might learn to fly! Your trouble may be your greatest opportunity!

Go down to the beach and watch the mountainous waves come crashing in and you will see two ways to meet a wave. The frightened, timid soul sees the monster wave looming, mounting, threatening. He turns, stumbling through the foamy shallows, and being too slow, he is overtaken, upset, flattened and sent sputtering in the surf by the liquid mountain. But farther in the deep you see a skillful rider of the surf who watches carefully the wave as it builds, swells, rises, and instead of running from the wave, he rides it! Instead of being flattened, he is lifted! Instead of being made low, he is raised high and carried far!

Every trouble has vast built-in opportunities to grow, to learn, to serve, or to be cleansed. Imagination can turn your bed of trouble into fruitful pasture. Your time of lying low can be your mourning of spiritual refreshment.

Whatever you do, don't make the mistake of thinking that your neighbor, with his seemingly untroubled life, is having all the good fortune! While your trouble may be a blessing in disguise, his blessing may be trouble hiding! Success has spoiled many a man. Security can stifle initiative and ambition. Prestige leads too quickly to pride. Power corrupts. Wealth brings with it vast temptations. Prosperity has more perils than poverty. I remember a magazine article by a famous actress, entitled, "My Beauty Was My Downfall." She later committed suicide. Why, that neighbor you envy for her untroubled life may be sick with boredom!

What must you do with your trouble? Sir Harry Lauder, a great Scottish comedian, received the tragic news that his son was killed in the First World War. He wrote these penetrating lines: "In a time like this there are three courses open to a man. He may give way to despair, sour upon the world, and become a grouch. He may endeavor to drown his sorrow in drink, in a life of waywardness and wickedness . . . or he may turn to God!"

These are the three choices open to you.

If you use your head, there is only one choice that makes any sense. Turn to God! Years later you will testify that once you were stopped in your tracks by what appeared to be an impossibly cruel mountain that blocked your path. You were mercilessly forced to climb it with bleeding hands and a breaking heart, until you reached the summit and there you found, hidden behind the rugged peak, the greenest little pasture encircling a heaven-pure mountain lake! The greenest pastures I have seen have been in the terrible mountain ranges—precious pockets painfully gouged out by grinding glaciers centuries before.

Let your troubles lead you to Christ, and they will prove to be the best friends you ever had!

#4—Learn and Live by the 60/40 Principle

I first learned this principle from one of my professors at Hope College in Holland, Michigan. "To avoid clashes and conflicts in marriage—never look upon marriage as a 50/50 proposition," he warned. "I give in 50 percent of the time—now it's your turn to give in" is a prescription for "keeping score" and is certain to generate tension," he predicted. "Again and again such a start-up mental attitude will focus on watching the scales to tip evenly always with exacting fairness," he explained. "The 50/50 principle operates more from a sense of justice than from a sense of affection. *Is this fair?* becomes more important than loving." This mind-set keeps an eye on the "fifty yard" line and both persons become more restrained, more cautious, less enthusiastic in their sharing as they approach this arbitrary boundary beyond which—for the sake of being treated fairly—they refuse to cross over.

"But live by the 60/40," was this professor's counsel. Each person agrees to "give in" 60 percent of the time and expects no more than 40 percent from the other partner. When both agree to give and share with this attitude, you avoid the deadlock on the arbitrary unyielding halfway mark. Instead of confrontation there is overlapping. The focus is on unselfish giving rather than on selfish getting. The heartbeat of the relationship is love—not justice.

Amazingly, justice prevails naturally when affection rules respectfully.

I've practiced this principle in my relationship of over forty years with my wife. I've extended the principle to many other arrangements. I'll never know how many times this has not only kept me from being unfair but also from being treated unfairly.

Living by the generous 60/40 principle gives the

goodness of God a chance to operate in situations where life is—or could easily become—unfair. If you make a mistake—make it on the side of mercy and God will be operating through your life to prove that *Life's not fair—but God is good!*

#5—THE LONG LOOK

Live by the *Overlook with the long look* attitude. Early in my life I encountered tough opposition from negative obstructionists. My normal, instinctive, impertinent gut reaction was to lash out, yield to anger and fight back. Or look for an excuse to split—and quit. The resistance I encountered seemed at the moment to be firmly entrenched. Then I ran into these lines from a Dr. Butler at Baylor University. "When things get rough—don't move! People and pressures shift but the soil remains the same no matter where you go." It set in my mental motions this reaction. "Don't quit. Don't split. Just sit. Wait. God will outlive, outlast, and outperform your opponent.

After thirty-six years on the job as founder and pastor of the Crystal Cathedral, I've been rewarded again and again and again. Critics passed away, moved on, left the scene, or were proven wrong, changed their minds, crossed over, and became supporters. All of which proved time and again (through patience and prayer) that *Life's not fair—but God is good!*

#6—FOCUS ON THE GOALS—NOT ON THE SHOALS

A ship can get hung up on the shoals unless it keeps its eyes on the goal—reaching port safely and successfully. Forget about the "raw deals," the "unfair treatment," and keep your mind set on the positive, constructive, creative goals. I've found great motivation

We Learn COURAGE
When We Face Danger;

We Learn PATIENCE
When We Endure Suffering,

We Learn TENDERNESS
When We Taste Pain,

We Discover True FRIENDSHIP
When False Ones
Forsake Us;

We Learn to Prize FREEDOM
When We Are In
Danger Of Losing It.

from these Bible verses, "Forgetting those things which
are behind and reaching forward to those things which
are ahead, I press toward the goal for the prize of the
upward call of God in Christ Jesus" (Phil. 3:13–14).

And for decades I kept these words of Jesus under
the glass top of my desk, "No one, having put his hand
to the plow, and looking back, is fit for the kingdom of
God" (Luke 9:62).

Unfairness doesn't really do serious damage unless
it causes me to take my eye off my goals. Remember—
there is no gain without pain! You simply keep on
keeping on and your accomplishments will mount
higher. Looking back you'll wonder how you managed
to hold on. You'll conclude that *life's not fair—but God is
good!*

#7—LOOK FOR THE LIGHT BEHIND EVERY SHADOW

Problems, challenges fall like dark shadows across
the path. That's life. Unfair treatment rises to block
the light and throw darkness along the way. But never
forget—there is a light behind every shadow. There
can be no shadow unless a light is shining somewhere.
There's a positive possibility in every adversity.

The tornado that struck our farm home couldn't
have hit at a worse time. All nine buildings were totally
destroyed. The farm machinery—the tools of our trade
—all were twisted into useless old iron in one hour of
destruction. Insurance? All we had added up to only
three thousand dollars. The mortgage was coming due
for payment.

My father did an amazing thing, as I look back on
it. He didn't blame God. He believed God. He could
have complained, "The non-religious farmer escaped.
I'm a believer and I get hit. It's not fair." Instead he
went to his bank with the insurance check in hand.

"I've come to make a payment on the mortgage. I can't pay it all, but I want to save the farm from fore-closure."

"But, Tony," the impressed banker replied, "You'll need this money to replace your lost machinery."

"I've decided I don't need these tools," Dad argued. "I'll just rent the land out for a year or two. If I apply most of the insurance money on the mortgage, will you give me a few more years to pay it off?"

The banker was deeply moved, inspired, actually. "You bet, Tony. We'll work with you."

The farm was refinanced. World War II broke out. Prices of farm products skyrocketed. The farm was saved—paid off in full—and allowed my father to spend his advanced years in relative prosperity!

The tornado was a blessing in disguise. Without it, the banker's attitude would have followed the custom-ary pattern, "Sorry, we'll have to take it over. If you can't make it now, you never will."

Even then I was learning this lesson: *Life's not fair—but God is good!*

#8—GOD IS GOOD—MAKE THIS REAL DISCOVERY TRULY PERSONAL IN YOUR LIFE!

We're not talking about religion—we're talking about a belief system that is a living, loving relationship between human beings and their Creator-God.

I was born and raised in a Holland Dutch colony in the State of Iowa in the United States of America. And in our colony, everybody shared the same simple Prot-estant faith, the Dutch Reformed faith.

Today, of course, with the advent of international technology, all of us are pulled out of our little colo-nies and we are exposed, like it or not, to a smorgas-bord of religious belief systems. Some attract us; some repel us; some confuse us and I hope at least one can be found that will inspire us.

I encountered one belief system quite by accident recently. It happens to be a system that I don't believe in, but I understand it is growing quite rapidly.

It happened when I was flying on a commercial airliner. The stewardess bent over as she placed a tray in front of me. As she did, the long, pear-shaped diamond that hung from a golden chain around her neck swung in front of my face, almost touching my nose. I had never seen a diamond that large, shaped so elegantly. Intuitively, instinctively, quite impulsively, I started to reach for it. When she saw my gesture, she pulled back, and with an alarming look, said, "Oh! Don't touch it!"

I quickly apologized. I said, "I'm sorry."

She said, "Don't touch it, because it's a crystal and the salt in your fingers will take some of the power out of it!"

Belief systems. There's quite a gamut available to us today. We will have to choose which one we will follow.

Where do they all come from? Some rise from MYTHS. Their origin lies in pure mythology. Others are the incarnation of internal EMOTIONAL PROJECTIONS. A person who is afraid of something sets up a belief system that he believes will protect him from those fears.

Some belief systems are just PERSONAL AGENDAS that people have created in order to give them a sense of power or an excuse to conquer more territory. Then there are belief systems that rise out of BOOKS that people wrote. Still others rise out of PHILOSOPHIES that seek to answer the ultimate questions. In the process, the search for answers takes the form of a religion.

There are other belief systems that originate with a

PERSON. That's why I am a Christian. That's my choice; that's my belief. It rises out of the life of Jesus Christ. *Who was He, anyway?*

There are few communities on this planet where the name of Jesus has never been heard. With the global century that we are not stepping into, as certain as there are satellites in the sky, as certain as there will be television sets in every hut, whether it's made of mud or glass or steel or grass, the name of Jesus cannot be ignored. HE'S the foundation of the belief system of the people you've met page after page throughout this book. It's a belief system that works wonders in wonderful people.

Whatever your faith—be fair to yourself! Get really informed on the facts about Jesus Christ. Whatever your faith—or lack of faith—face up to this fact: "Jesus Christ, I've got to get to know You better. Amen."

Now Then, Who Is Jesus?

Jesus, Himself, raised the question. He said to Peter, "Who do people say that I am?"

Peter replied, "Some say You're one of the prophets. And some say You're Elijah come back."

Jesus then asked, "Peter, who do YOU say that I am?"

Peter said, "You are Christ, the Son of the living God."

John the Baptist also sought to know the identity of Jesus. He had heard the reports that concerned Jesus. He heard about His works and he heard about His claims. John was a prophet of high regard, so he sent some of his disciples to go to Jesus with one specific question, "Are You the One that we are waiting for? Are you the Messiah?"

Jesus said, "Go back and tell John—the blind see,

the lame walk, the deaf speak, the poor are liberated. I am He."

When the religious authorities heard about this claim of Christ's—to be the Son of God, to be the Messiah—they brought Him to trial. These theologians and sophisticated religious people held court. They likewise asked Him the question: "Are You claiming to be the Christ?"

He replied, "I am."

That claim was considered to be blasphemy—punishable by death. Only the Roman governor could issue the death penalty. So the religious leaders brought Jesus before Pilate. Again the question was raised, this time by Pontius Pilate, "Do You claim to be the Christ, the Son of the living God?"

Jesus claimed once again, this time in a Roman court, this time knowing that His words would be a death sentence, "I am He!"

Pilate then uttered a second question. It is a question that each person must answer. Pilate asked, "What then, shall I do with this Jesus, who is called Christ?"

No matter what your belief system is, whether you're an atheist or a humanist, you too have come to terms with the historical person called Jesus Christ.

John Stuart Mill, the great philosopher, said, *"You can never accept any position until you have rejected all of the alternatives."*

If you want to be an intelligent, rational-thinking, logical, educated, academic intellectual, you cannot ignore the issue of Christ and who He was and what you will do with Him. You either accept—or reject Him.

So ask yourself these questions: 1. *What do you think of Christ's CHARACTER?* 2. *What do you think of His CLAIMS?* 3. *What do you think of His CROSS?* 4. *What do you think of His CONVERTS?* 5. *What do you think of His*

"MORE THAN CONQUERING" spirit that He infuses into human lives?

What Do You Think of His Character?

Start here. Look at the man, Jesus. No one ever faulted Him in His trial or in His death. No one ever accused Him of an unethical or an immoral act. There have been anti-Christian and anti-Jewish writers of this century, who have fictionalized and fabricated shameful and immoral accounts that have no basis in fact at all. Jesus still has enemies today. The truth is this: No one in His day could ever find fault with Him. Even those who wanted Him out of the way couldn't accuse Him of anything. His character was impeccable.

Look at the quality of His life. What do you think of that? Jesus did not accept everything He was taught as a boy. Jesus rejected some of the teachings that were indoctrinated into Him. Specifically He was taught, "An eye for an eye and a tooth for a tooth." To this day, there are prominent religions that still accept this teaching as truth.

Jesus brought a new message, "We've all been taught," He said, *"An eye for an eye and a tooth for a tooth; but I say to you, Love your enemies."* Jesus taught forgiveness. Mercy. Redemption. This is the hallmark of His life and of the beliefs of those who follow Him.

What Do You Think of His Claims?

What are you going to do with this person called Jesus? What are you going to do with His claims?

He claimed:

- "I am the light of the world."
- "I am the bread of life."

- "I am the door, if any man enter by Me, he shall be saved."
- "I am the Christ, the Son of the living God."

When I was a student at college, I looked into these claims. I became interested in philosophy and comparative religions. I've searched all of the religions. It was like leaving an island shore in a little boat and cruising through stormy waters, not knowing where I went, but hugging close to the line of the shore itself, until finally one day I got out of the boat and discovered that I had gone full circle around the island and was now stepping back to the point where I had STARTED. But during that journey, I thought of other faiths. I questioned the deity of Jesus Christ.

I could dismiss it as a myth until I came face to face with this unanswerable reality: *He claimed to be God coming to earth.*

He wasn't a braggart or a boastful person. He merely claimed it. And when they nailed Him on it, He died for that claim.

No psychologist, no psychiatrist has ever seen any neuroticism or insecurity when they analyzed the personality of Jesus. That means that He's the kind of person you can trust. The conclusion then is this: Either He was telling the truth or He was the world's worst liar. But emotionally secure and mentally healthy people like Jesus do not lie. They don't have to. He backed His claim with His life.

What Do You Think of His Cross?

History will never, ever be able to forget it. Thirty-three years old. A truly beautiful human being. They crucified Him as a common criminal—between two other authentic criminals. Horrible. Humiliating.

From the time they drove the nails through His hands until He breathed His last breath seven agonizing, horrific hours passed.

They jeered at Him, "He saved others; Himself He cannot save" (Matt. 27:42).

They jabbed Him. A soldier plunged a sword into His side. Water and blood flowed out.

He was a good man.

He didn't deserve this.

Write this sentence boldly beneath His cross:

"LIFE'S NOT FAIR!"

Carve the letters in granite. Paint them in red. Don't ever let history forget it!

Miracle of miracles! He did not lash out at His enemies.

His dying words were: "Father, forgive them, for they do not know what they do" (Luke 23:34).

I could believe in a God like that!! I'd be a fool not to!

They took His body down. Carefully. Wrapped it in cloth and buried it. A huge stone sealed the tomb. Roman soldiers were ordered by Pilate to guard the burial place, "to make sure no one would steal the body and start a religious myth that He's been resurrected."

Then the Roman seal was fixed across the stone so no one could possibly move the stone without breaking the seal. That would stop would-be thieves. For breaking a Roman seal was tantamount to murder. Anyone caught would be executed. Likewise, any Roman soldier caught napping on the watch would be summarily killed as well. You can be sure the soldiers would not fall asleep on this job.

Then it happened.

Facts and mysteries happened:

Fact: The seal was broken!

Fact: The stone was rolled away!

Fact: The body disappeared!

Mystery: Frightened, scattered, petrified disciples who had fled the scene fearing they might be next were alone in a room when Jesus reappeared! There wasn't a single doubt among them—except for Thomas, "Let me touch You—and I'll believe!"

Jesus answered, "Here, Thomas, are My hands. Put your fingers in these holes."

Thomas did as he was told. And Doubting Thomas became Thomas the Believer.

Something history-shattering happened that first Easter morning! The mystery of the miraculous resurrection!

Go back now to the empty cross—read the words, "LIFE'S NOT FAIR."

But wait! It's Easter! Finish the sentence, "BUT GOD IS GOOD!"

Proof? Just look at the converts! So . . .

What Do You Think of His Converts?

There is a little town in Pennsylvania. The story is told by historian Clarence McCartney of a Baptist pastor who had a terrible problem with a difficult member of his congregation during the time of the American Revolution. One day that difficult young man joined the army of General George Washington. He betrayed the Army and was sentenced to be executed. The Baptist pastor walked seventy miles, hoping to pray with the young man before his execution.

The pastor arrived at the army camp. He spoke to General Washington and appealed for forgiveness and pardon. General Washington heard him out, then said, "I am very sorry, but I can do nothing for your friend."

The pastor said, "My friend? My friend? He's not my friend! He's my enemy."

When General George Washington heard that, he said, "If you would walk that far through the snow and the ice to save an enemy, then I will pardon him."

This gift called pardon, forgiveness, grace, is shocking! Incredible! You will not find such grace of human spirit portrayed anywhere as vividly as in the history of Christianity.

Before you dismiss Jesus Christ you have to decide upon those whose lives He has changed. Of course there are the hypocrites—every belief system has them. But before you condemn the faith because of its sins remember this: Christianity has the distinction of being the one religion that more than any other belief system spends billions of dollars to try to talk Gentiles, sinners, and bad people into joining its ranks!

So the Christian church with the forgiving, saving, life-redeeming spirit of Jesus became the God-ordered belief system designed to appeal to hopeless cases! "The Christian church is not a museum for saints—it's a hospital for sinners," the Episcopal priest Sam Shoemaker said (who by the way was then an anonymous author of the Twelve Steps of Alcoholics Anonymous! A contribution of Jesus Christ).

What Do You Think of the "More Than Conquering" Power that Christ Infuses by His Living Spirit Into People Today?

Again and again he conquers the Doubting Thomas by coming into skeptical and intelligent minds with born again "belief."

St. Paul said, "We are more than conquerors through Him who loved us" (Rom. 8:37).

There is something more than winning over life's

injustice—it's turning our opponents into partners. There's something more important than victory, conquest and the destruction of our enemies. What's better than that? It's restoration! Rebuilding! Reconstruction! Helping and healing our adversaries to become beautiful human beings again. That's called redemption. It's also called—authentic Christianity!

How can we live in an unfair world?

Only with the goodness of God in our heart—that's how.

More than conquerors—redeemers! Discovering something more than success—significance!

The late Dr. Louis Evans was my friend. For years he was the pastor at First Presbyterian Church in Hollywood, California. He told me of one of Beverly Hills' wealthiest and most successful doctors. But fame and fortune left something spiritually lacking in the surgeon's life. Honestly—sincerely—privately he became a "seeker." He studied and he learned about Jesus Christ. He became overwhelmed by the love of the beautiful person and accepted the Christian faith.

FROM SUCCESS TO SIGNIFICANCE

"How can I really make a difference for Christ? How can I serve Him?" the doctor asked. The questions were soon to be answered. The Korean War was over now—"I can volunteer as a surgeon in that devastated land," he thought. The Presbyterian mission in Korea accepted him. Years later the pastor who introduced the doctor to Jesus Christ went to Korea to visit him. "I'm doing surgery today, Dr. Evans. You're welcome to watch, although it might not be too pleasant."

"I'd love to!" Evans replied.

I recall Dr. Evans account: "For seven hot hours, in a steamy, makeshift surgical room, filled with obnoxious human odors, I watched the doctor at work. It was astonishing. Finally finished, he smiled and led me to his little cramped office. He excused himself to clean up and came to sit at the splintered desk. "I'm curious," Dr. Evans said, "What would you have been paid for this operation in America?"

"A bundle! Yes—a bundle. I can tell you that!"

"And what were you paid—here—today?"

He laughed again, reached for a dented coin on the desk and said, "For starters, I was paid this! She came in, the poor creature, for an exam. She couldn't live long without surgery. 'What will the operation cost, Doctor?' she asked. Handing me the coin, she added, 'Will this cover it?'

"I took it. Seriously I said, 'Why, that's exactly what I was going to charge—thank you!'" He fondled the coin. He looked Dr. Evans square in the eye and said, "For starters I got this—but the big payoff was . . ." His eyes became soft. They glistened. He held his hands up and said, "For the past seven hours I had the wonderful, wonderful feeling that these hands were the healing hands of Jesus Christ."

Fair pay? Of course!

My good friend, Dr. Peale tells the story of a famous surgeon who was a member of his church, The Marble Collegiate Church in New York City. Dr. Peale was asked to say the prayer at a retirement luncheon for this surgeon. As Dr. Peale sat next to the surgeon at lunch he asked him, "Doctor, is there one surgery in your entire career that stands out above the others?"

The doctor replied immediately, "Oh, yes! I'll never forget it. She was just a frail little girl. Five years old. There was only a ten per cent chance for her survival. I went to see her before they gave her the anesthesia since I always see my patients before surgery. I looked at this poor little girl, so small, so thin, gray-faced, dying. I said, 'Hi, Annie.'

"She said, 'What's going to happen to me, doctor?'

"I explained as well as I knew how, 'Well, some nurses will give you something that will make you sleep very deeply.'

"Her eyes brightened and she said soberly, 'Then I guess it's time to pray.'

" 'Oh?'

" 'Yes,' she said, 'Mommy says, always pray before you go to sleep. May I pray now, doctor?' He nodded. Holding the doctor's hand, she said, 'Jesus, tender shepherd hear me. Watch Your little lamb, I pray. Through the darkness, be Thou near me. Keep me safe till break of day and bless the doctor too. Cause he's got troubles too.'

"She didn't know the troubles I was having in my home. It just broke me up. Embarrassed, I turned my back to her and to the nurses and acted like I was washing at the sink. But in that moment I prayed, 'Oh, God, if ever these ten fingers save a life, Dear Lord, help me to save this one.' In that moment, I felt God's spirit and presence.

"The prayer was answered, she survived. The surgery was a success, but the biggest success, Dr. Peale, was that God came into my life."

What are YOU going to do with Jesus? I've chosen to believe that He was who He said He was. We live in a very uncertain world. The global community that is emerging is changing rapidly. Life is uncertain. It is difficult. Frequently it is unfair. How comforting to know that there is a God who will have the last word. God is good and His plans for us are good. When we follow Him, He will show us the right way to go. It may not be an easy way—but it will be the right way.

And when you come to the end of your life, the end of the journey, you will know that your life has counted. You will have the assurance that you have made a difference. You will know beyond a shadow of a doubt that God is good. You know because He is your friend. He has walked beside you. He has led you. He has guided you. He has strengthened you. At times He has carried you. At all times He has loved you and believed in you.

I shall never forget the airplane ride when I occupied a seat next to Bear Bryant. He was a great football coach. He approached me on the plane and introduced himself. I invited him to sit down. I said, "It's always nice to meet another good Christian."

He responded, "Well, I don't know if I'm a good Christian. I smoke and I drink."

I said, "Any other reason why you're not a Christian?"

"Well," he said, "I'm not sure I believe everything in the Bible."

I said, "Oh? Any other reasons?"

"Yes. I've never had the feeling. I understand if you become a Christian, you're supposed to have a big feeling; I've never had the feeling."

I said, "I don't know if there's a heaven; I don't know if there's a hell; I don't know what's beyond this life, except one thing: a lot of people are gone ahead of me. They know a lot more about it than I do. And number one is Jesus." I said, "If you died tonight, would you be afraid of the darkness out there? Would you be afraid to die?"

He said, "Yes, I think so."

I looked him in the eye. He looked as though he desperately wanted something and Someone he could believe in. I said, "Well, let me give you your ticket to heaven, whatever heaven is and wherever it is. Jesus believed in it, and I think He knew something I don't know. Let me give you a ticket to heaven."

He said, "Can you do that?"

"Sure." Then I wrote a Bible verse, the words of Jesus, "And the one who comes to me I will by no means cast out" (John 6:37). Then I printed the words: "I accept that today." I drew a line, and said, "Sign your name."

He said in his gravelly voice, "I don't know if I should sign that."

I said, "I don't know if I can be sure this plane is gonna land, either! Coach, that's what you call faith."

He looked at me and said, "I'll sign it!"

I'll never forget watching him fold up that piece of paper. Then he reached into his pocket and he got out his worn leather billfold, held together with rubber bands. He took the rubber bands off and he put the Bible verse with his signature in the billfold. And he said, "O.K., this will be my ticket to heaven."

I told the story one Sunday, many months later. It aired on a Sunday morning across America. The next day, Coach Bear Bryant died suddenly. I was very happy to know that he had his ticket to heaven.

JESUS IS THE SAME—YESTERDAY, TODAY, AND FOREVER

Dr. Irwin J. Lubbers, one of the great educators in the United States of America, was the president of Hope College when I was a student there. Occasionally, he shared his faith with the students. He did not care to share it too publicly, but with his students he opened himself and related to us a dramatic story that changed his life.

Dr. Lubbers told us about the day when he was in a car driving with his little boy Don. They hit a piece of ice; the car spun out of control. It landed upside down in the ditch. Dr. Lubbers was unconscious. He awoke from his unconsciousness briefly to find himself thrown from the car, lying in the snow in the arms of his little boy.

His son Don was crying and praying, "Dear Jesus, don't let my daddy die! Dear Jesus, don't let my daddy die!"

"Then," Dr. Lubbers said, "I saw the presence of Jesus. I am a secularist; I am a humanist; I am a scientist; I am an educator; I am a relationist—but I am also a Christian."

I am only one of millions and millions and millions and millions of people who for two thousand years claim to *know* and to *have met*, and claim to have a positive relationship through faith and prayer with this living human/divine person, named Jesus Christ. He is alive. He's the same, yesterday, today, and forever. Occasionally He breaks through dramatically and crunches and crashes into people's lives and performs dramatic miracles. Other times He supports quietly, leading, walking silently along, giving the courage to carve a new life.

Of course, it's true—LIFE'S NOT FAIR—But GOD IS GOOD! Jesus Christ is proof enough of that! Pray this prayer, and the end of this book will become a new beginning:

Prayer

Dear Jesus, I've got to get to know You better. Please help me!

I can feel my spiritual and emotional walls

crack. I can hear old chains break. I can feel my heart opening like a heavy old door whose ancient seals have just begun to break. I can sense the footsteps of Jesus walking into my life. I am beginning to experience the joy of a soul that is being saved, a life that is being born again. Thank You, Lord! Life's not fair, but God is good. Amen.

About the Author

Dr. Robert H. Schuller is the founder and senior minister of the Crystal Cathedral in Garden Grove, California. From his pulpit, Dr. Schuller preaches his powerful message of positive thinking each week to the largest television congregation in the world on his program, "The Hour of Power."

In 1989 Dr. Schuller received the distinguished Horatio Alger Award. He has written more than twenty-eight books and has received numerous awards for his creative communications style.

His previous books include *Believe in the God Who Believes in You*, *The Be (Happy) Attitudes*, *Success Is Never Ending, Failure Is Never Final*, *Tough Times Never Last, but Tough People Do!*, *Tough-Minded Faith for Tender-Hearted People*, and *Life's Not Fair, but God Is Good*.

"May the Lord
      touch your heart
            with his finger of love
and leave a fingerprint
            no one can rub off."

—ROBERT H. SCHULLER,
from *Be Happy You Are Loved*

WORDS OF INSPIRATION FROM ROBERT H. SCHULLER

____26458-3	The Be (Happy) Attitudes	$5.99/$7.99 Canada
____28867-9	Believe in the God Who Believes in You	$5.99/$7.99
____28182-8	Success is Never Ending, Failure is Never Final	$5.99/$7.99
____27332-9	Tough Times Never Last, but Tough People Do!	$5.99/$7.50
____24704-2	Tough-Minded Faith for Tender-Hearted People	$5.99/$7.99
____56167-7	Life's Not Fair, but God Is Good	$5.99/$7.99

DR. NATHANIEL
BRANDEN

*The psychologist who awakened America's
consciousness to the importance of self-esteem
provides simple techniques you can start practicing
as early as today to dramatically transform the
way you think and feel about yourself!*

___26814-7 HONORING THE SELF $6.99/$8.99 Canada

___26646-2 HOW TO RAISE YOUR SELF-ESTEEM $6.50/$8.99

___27555-0 THE PSYCHOLOGY OF

                ROMANTIC LOVE $5.99/$7.99

___37439-7 THE SIX PILLARS OF SELF-ESTEEM $13.95/$19.95

Ask for these books at your local bookstore or use this page to order.

Please send me the books I have checked above. I am enclosing $____(add $2.50 to
cover postage and handling). Send check or money order, no cash or C.O.D.'s, please.

Name _____

Address _____

City/State/Zip _____

Send order to: Bantam Books, Dept. NB 3, 2451 S. Wolf Rd., Des Plaines, IL 60018
Allow four to six weeks for delivery.
Prices and availability subject to change without notice.   NB 3 5/96

*The Inspirational Bestseller That Has Led
Thousands to the Fulfillment of Their Desires
Through the Art of Mental Energy and Affirmation*

Creative Visualization

— Shakti Gawain —

Creative Visualization is a workbook for using mental energy to transform and greatly improve health, beauty, prosperity, loving relationships, and the fulfillment of all your desires. Popular inspirational teacher Shakti Gawain provides easy-to-follow exercises, meditations, affirmations, and other techniques to tap into the natural goodness and beauty in all of life—to give you the ability to become a radiant being—to make positive ideas and concepts a total reality.

___27044-3 $5.99/$7.99 in Canada